Ernie Hoare

ERNIE

ERNIE

E Hoare

ATHENA PRESS
LONDON

ERNIE
Copyright © E Hoare 2005

All Rights Reserved

ISBN 1 84401 539 4

First Published 2005 by
ATHENA PRESS
Queen's House, 2 Holly Road
Twickenham TW1 4EG
United Kingdom

Printed for Athena Press

Contents

Part One

Young Ernie

FIRST DAY AT SCHOOL, loved it. Loved it ever since. The reason being, I was pretty bright and always top of class. Hated to leave. I was presented with the school badge for being top of the school, even beating the top girl. But I had to leave school to bring in a few shillings toward the family coffers. Aged fourteen years, I had no chance of going on to university – reason: family poor.

I was born 12 August 1921 in the days of the economic depression, number seven of twelve children. Dad scraped a living by window cleaning. Mum worked her fingers off, taking in laundry for those lucky enough to pay a few measly shillings. One penny for a shirt, half penny for collar starched and pressed. I turned the handle of the big mangle whilst Mum fed clothes into wooden rollers.

Prior to that, we had to get fire going under the copper boiler – burn anything we could get hold of – old boots, bits and pieces. Blankets and sheets were the hardest to wring out. Dad occasionally brought home a carpet to beat. I turned the clothes over now and then with a copper stick. Mum used soda and a substance called bluebag to get the clothes clean, together with Sunlight soap. All this on top of the family wash and ironing.

She sewed my school badge on my bathing costume. Couldn't afford a blazer. When I was twelve years of age, Mum got into debt to buy me my first pair of long trousers from the tallyman – thanks Mum. Getting too big for shorts. My last pair was past repair – a hole in the backside, the tail of my shirt poking through.

Let me talk a bit about Mum. She was the mainstay and disciplinarian and doled out the occasional clump around the ear when called for. When we got a bit out of hand, she would only have to say, 'Wait till your father comes home', which would put the fear of God into us. Very rarely, he would take off his belt to us. His trouser belt was a two-inch ex-Army belt. Just use your imagination to see what that threat did to us. When Dad came home, we all did the disappearing act.

When she got us kids off to school and out of her way, she set to work – either hearth-stoning the front step of Portland Stone or maybe blackening the kitchen stove and polishing the brassware. Occasionally to brighten the room, she would dye the curtains a different colour.

Believe it or not she did all the painting and wallpapering. No wonder she had to loosen off her corsets, or stays, as we called them. These were body garments stiffened with whalebone and pulled tight with criss-crossed laces. To keep herself slim when she wanted to go out, she would get one of us kids to help tighten up the laces. This meant putting your knee into the small of her back and pulling the laces as tight as she could bear. They had pride, these Victorian women. No wonder they often fainted with these things on, plus the fact that they were half starved most of the time. Very seldom did we see Mum with her beautiful long hair down. After brushing and combing, the locks were twisted and pinned into a knot at the back to her head, called a bun.

Where were we? Oh yes, let's get to cooking!

Mum would make something out of next to nothing. She would send me down to the local butcher to get sixpenny-worth of bacon pieces; these she would make into a suet, parsley and bacon roll. With such a big family, it was essential to use a very big boiling pot. Once made up into a roll and covered in muslin cloth, it would be steam-boiled for hours. Very tasty. With the remainder of the suet, she would make a spotty dog sweet pudding with custard.

The highlight of the week, money permitting, was the Sunday roast dinner. Roast beef, roast and boiled spuds, Yorkshire pudding and sprouts. For tea, Dad would bring home a pint of winkles bought from outside of the pub. Now it was the turn of we kids to do something. Armed with a pin each, our job was to remove the winkles' eyes and, with a deft twist of the wrist, extricate the winkles from their shells. These were put into a slice of bread, margarine and watercress. Sometimes we could use our own mustard and cress which had been cultivated on a piece of wet flannel cloth and harvested when about an inch high with a pair of scissors. Also, Dad would bring home biscuits, especially for the youngest to teeth on. That would take care of Sunday.

Poor old girl. Mum was sometimes up to all hours cutting and sewing a pair of trousers cut down from Dad's cast-offs. Her eyes would be nearly popping out of her head through lack of sleep. She would spit on the smoothing iron to make sure our clothes were not scorched. My elder sisters did similar with curling tongs for hair.

At eleven years old I started a paper round to earn a few pence. Mum awakened me about 7 a.m. to grab a slice of bread and margarine and a cup of tea. Usually I went to newsagent's shop well before opening hours and would lie down on bundles of newspapers and drop off to sleep even when it was freezing. Good man, the newsagent. He numbered all the papers and magazines to be delivered on my round. On Saturdays after I had collected all monies from customers on my round, Charlie the boss would give me sixpence extra to see Brentford play football. One penny tram fare and one penny return. Four pence entrance fee at Griffin Park. I had to hang on for dear life on the vastly overcrowded tram. Once inside the ground the men looked after us kids by passing us over their heads past the crush barriers to sit near the touchline. Happy days, the school days were for me. I entered a competition from the boys' magazine, *Hotspur* to send in a copy of handwriting, long-hand and script spelling and numerals, etc. I won a nice football, which gave me a big head.

Now, Mondays were traditionally washdays. So for quickness, the main meal was bubble and squeak, the remains of Sunday's repast fried up. The rest of the week, we would take pot luck except for Friday. Maybe when we could afford it we had fish and chips on the menu. A twopenny piece of fish and pennyworth of chips. The twopenny piece of fish was invariably either cod, haddock or huss, i.e. rock salmon. If you could spare three pence, plaice was the tasty fish. When we were hungry during the week, there was always a bag of crackling to be had for a halfpenny. The hungriest days were when Dad could not earn a few bob window cleaning because of rain or frost. Then it was bread and margarine topped with mashed spuds, or sugar, tinned milk or Bovril. When you were hungry, it all tasted good. Egg and chips were a favourite. Eggs were relatively cheap, namely one shilling for a baker's dozen of thirteen. Walking down the street, a man with a tray on his head would ring a bell, shouting out, 'Muffins, muffins, lovely muffins!'

In those days (the years up to 1938) there were several street vendors calling out their wares, such as the paraffin man, rag and bone man and ice cream man. The milkman came round four times a day measuring out the milk from a churn on a horse-drawn cart. There was the tinker who would shout out, 'scissors to grind!' and there was the rag and bone man – for a few rags we were given a goldfish. We could get a halfpenny for each empty jam jar. Nothing was wasted. A bundle of old newspapers would get you a couple of coppers from the fishmonger. Empty beer and Tizer bottles got you a penny – all for recycling. Rags went to the paper manufacturer. The organ grinder with his little monkey would pay us a visit now and then. The newspaper boy and the local bobby came twice a day. The name 'bobby' was derived from Sir Robert Peel, founder of the police force – sometimes the police were called 'Peelers'. We scarpered sharply with his appearance and his rolled-up heavy cape. I had experienced a whack from his cape when he caught me up an apple tree, scrumping apples from Manns' orchard.

Mum's thirteenth child was stillborn – unlucky thirteen. The doctor told my eldest brother to bury it in a shoebox at the end of the garden. Another of Mum's babies was born with a cowl over the head, some sort of membrane. It was considered very lucky and a seaman would give anything to possess one. It was considered that a cowl protected them from drowning – sailors being very superstitious. It was the normal thing to have large families in Victorian times – Queen Victoria was reported to have had fifteen children – I don't know how many survived.

Mum, having lost her baby at birth, was full of mother's milk. What did she do? She went to visit a women she knew who could not breast-feed her baby and became a so-called wet nurse for her.

Isleworth, our neighbouring town, was a very religious place, a cross being the emblem on the Borough insignia. Every year a Catholic procession would take place. Mum made sure we all attended. What a show! What with all the banners and image of the Virgin Mary in the procession and the priests swinging incense, all of the novice nuns dressed immaculately in white. It was a show to behold. Although she did not speak with an Irish brogue, I think Mum must have had an Irish connection because her maiden name was Keane.

Going back to my childhood reminiscences.

Saving my pocket money earned from the paper round, I bought myself a pair of shoes. My old ones were full of holes and I had to stick cardboard inside in the hope of keeping dampness out. Some hope!

Before that, the only time I can remember having a pair of boots that didn't leak was when my best mate's Dad gave me a pair that he had repaired with a piece of motor tyre. Sadly this schoolmate Jim went down in the battleship *Hood* whilst I was in the Royal Air Force. I lost several of my mates during the War.

Quite near where we lived, there was an encampment of gypsies with the gypsy caravans. We were often visited by them selling us their homemade clothes-pegs or so-called lucky heather. It was considered provident to purchase something from them or they would put a gypsy curse upon you. Back then, they were encamped near to what became Mogden Sewage Works. Unfortunately for my eldest brother, he ventured too near them and was duly dumped into the then open cesspool. He was fortunately rescued by some kindly man, and for his good deed he earned the name of 'Cacker'.

This cesspit was adjacent to Mogden Lane. I mean a proper lane with hedges on both sides. This was a favourite place to go bird nesting, i.e. stealing the eggs from the nest – I had quite a collection of them. All you had to do was to pinprick a small hole at both ends of the egg and blow out the yolk. Then place them in an empty matchbox lined with cotton wool. I also had a collection of butterflies. These I caught with a small fishing net. Where did I keep them? At the end of our garden in the field there was an old abandoned horse-drawn tram. I spent a lot of time in it pinning my butterflies to the woodwork.

Incidentally this field was given to my Granddad by Lord Kilmoray, a great friend of my grandfather. My grandfather was too lazy to fence it in – hence it was being used as a dumping ground. Land was not very valuable in those days. A market gardener squatted on it and, in time, claimed it. An air raid shelter was built on it during the War. Soon after the War it was sold for a million pounds – silly old Granddad. Granddad was a master builder who built the family house and five more in our road (Haliburton Road, St Margarets, East Twickenham). Grandfather, a wealthy man at that time, used to hob-nob with the elite, going to all the horse-race meetings and gambling very heavily, eventually frittering away all the family fortune. He even had to sell the family house and rent it back from the new owners. Let that be a lesson to you. That is why my parents had to work so hard bringing up a family.

These gypsy women I mentioned before used to sit outside a public house in Isleworth on a bench with a table, quaffing their pint of Porter and smoking their clay pipes. The nursing mothers thought it the normal thing to breastfeed their offspring to the view of any passer-by: my mother would never dream of doing it in public.

I remember seeing a little old granny, a local character with a very long shirt reaching down to her ankles, standing astride a road drain and relieving herself. I assume she never wore bloomers. Maybe she was incontinent.

We lived not far from the lock and weir bridge, straddling the River Thames between Richmond and St. Margarets. This bridge was a toll bridge, which would cost you a penny to cross over from one side to the other. We lads, not wanting to pay this toll, used to bunk over sharpish when the toll collector was distracted serving people using the opposing walkway. It was either that or walking a fair distance along Ducks Walk to Richmond Bridge.

When I was a lad, about ten or eleven, they started to build the Chertsey Road Bridge. Now my eldest sister's husband owned a barge and was contracted to work on the construction. One day a workman threw a bolt at a seagull and downed it in the river; that so incensed my brother-in-law, he knocked the hell out of this cruel workman and brought the seagull home to us. We tried to feed her on fish. But Biddy, as we called her, died shortly afterwards. Having internal injuries, she would not keep her food down.

A little way upstream of Richmond is the town of Teddington. This is where the sea's twice daily tidal influence upon the waters ended. Hence Teddington's name is derived from this occurrence. Namely, tide/end/town. There is a nice pub there called the Tide End.

The Richmond Lock and weir toll bridge was built to have control of the water. For those who do not know what that means I will try to enlighten you. If there were no locks to control the flow of water, the water would simply flow into the sea. The biggest of the locks being at Richmond, the last bastion to contain the fresh waters from the upper reaches. It is quite interesting to watch the working of the machinery – raising and lowering the huge sluice gates. These gates were lowered into the riverbed. In my youth the machinery mechanism had to be applied by the lock-keeper and his assistant. Nowadays it is motorised. At high tide, the gates were lowered and it was soon noticed that the water level downstream began to drop. To keep the Thames navigable, a lock was the means used to raise or lower the boats to the required level up or down as the case may be. A fee must be paid for the service. The lock-keeper used a long handled net to receive it.

Unfortunately, one day Sammy the seal was trapped under a sluice gate. After he was retrieved from his watery grave he was stuffed and preserved and later put on show at Wate's shipyard.

I was fascinated watching the many steamers and pleasure craft using the lock to go up or down stream. The riverbed had to be continually dredged to have a navigable passage for the larger boats. Now and then a steamer would get stranded and would have to wait for the incoming tide to refloat it.

(Now that my cat Susie has stopped pestering me I shall resume this narrative).

One day when I was about fifteen (about 1936), four of us likely lads hired a skiff-boat to row upstream and pull in at Marble Hill landing stage. After showing off and giving the girls a ride in the boat, it was now time to return the boat to its owner. This was easier said than done. We had left Marble Hill later than planned. Now the tide had turned and we had to row hard against it. When we got back as far as the ice drome, we realised we were sinking fast. Hurriedly we pulled into the shore and tied up to an overhanging willow tree and scrambled ashore. Needless to say, we never went back to retrieve our five shilling deposit. I believe we may have holed the boat on the shingle at Marble Hill. The next day we saw a Thames Policeboat towing the boat back to its rightful owners.

I became quite a crack shot with a handmade catapult. Now to make a catapult, firstly you need a Y-shaped branch of a willow tree. No problem there, as there are plenty of them growing along the banks of the Thames on the Surrey side towards Kew Gardens. Having selected the best branch, I would cut it down with my trusty bowie knife and trim it with my boy-scout knife. The next thing required was some elastic, which I would perhaps pinch from my sisters' drawers. Failing that, we discovered that the inside of a golf ball was made up with yards of elastic. Another alternative was the inner tube of a bicycle. To obtain a golf ball, we had to steal one from the golf course adjoining Old Deer Park: nip out sharply from a hiding place when you heard the shout of 'Fore', pinch the ball and scarper. Now all that was needed was the leather tongue of an old boot, plus some string to bind the handle. There was no shortage of ammo as there was an endless supply of pebbles from the Thames. Later we used ball bearings. My favourite target was to ring the bell in the tower of the local riverside church. It was considered not good to aim at a sitting duck.

The ha-ha running alongside the Thames to irrigate Kew Gardens was alive with fish tiddlers and newts. We spent hours fishing for them. The water of the ha-ha came from the Thames and trapped the fish by a non-return valve.

Once or twice a year, the sluice gates were left open and at low tide the water was allowed to flow into the sea, draining the lower reaches and exposing the river bed; it being possible then to cross over from one side to the other without having to pay a toll. The reason for this operation was to expose all the bridge foundations for examination and possible repair. The boat owners took advantage of this, when their boats were stranded, to inspect the hulls of their craft. This was an ideal opportunity for anyone to go searching for anything on the riverbed. Apart from all the usual trash like old bikes and prams, occasionally we found objects worth keeping, such as Roman coins or an anchor. It was surprising the various objects you would find.

Another one of our escapades was to build a raft of empty oil drums, lashed together with rope and bits of wood for paddles. We launched the raft from the end of a garden backing onto the River Crane which flowed into the Thames. Bearing in mind that none of us could swim at that time we were very adventurous, wouldn't you say! It was a bit scary when we were swept into the Thames. We managed to tie up at an island midstream and awaited a favourable turning of the tide to take us back to our starting point.

We were so lucky living in this area of the Thames, being within walking distance of such places as Hampton Court, Kew Gardens, Sion Park, Marble Hill, Richmond and Bushey Parks. The big drawback is living so near to Heathrow Airport with all the noise and traffic conditions. However, in my boyhood we were not subject to this annoyance. Progress! Who needs it?

During my early youth, Mum related an incident to me: arriving at the doorstep of our meagre abode, a very posh lady came to visit. Apparently she was some sort of relative of my wayward grandfather. She arrived in all her finery and stepped down from her horse-drawn carriage. No doubt her visit was to commiserate with my grandfather (or to gloat) over his misfortunes. I very much doubt that she came to offer financial assistance, for we continued to live in poverty.

Another little story comes to mind. My very good friend Jimmy and I had another little task to perform in his father's bakery. When the dough had risen in their long wooden troughs and had pushed the lids off all the dough full of air had to be punched to release said air. Jimmy and I rolled up our sleeves and set to. We were also set to cleaning out the huge dough mixer which was big enough to enter and clean the inside. Another one of our jobs was to brush hot cross buns with sugar wash and to put crosses on them with a wooden tool. I did these chores quite happily, especially during the cold weather. I would often be given some stale cakes for my efforts to take home to my grateful Mum.

I started smoking when I was about eleven years old. I made a pipe out of an old acorn hollowed out, the stem being a hollow piece of straw. For tobacco a stub of a fag was used. In those days most men and boys smoked but very few women did. Every film we saw, the hero and sometimes the heroine would be smoking, cowboys rolling their own fags, etc. We were blissfully ignorant of the dire consequences of inhaling the deadly smoke. Later generations, despite all the warnings, still smoke the noxious weed. After thirty years of this filthy habit and being completely hooked, I managed through sheer willpower to kick it. When desperate for a fag I would stuff a sweet, namely a 'Spangle' into my gob until the pangs receded.

This wally, Sir Walter Raleigh – you know, the one who, to ingratiate himself with Queen Elizabeth I, threw his cape over a puddle so that she would not dirty her shoes – he brought back with him two items, in particular, the tobacco plant and the potato plant. Both of which, in my opinion, caused many a death. Firstly, the Irish populations suffered horribly when blight wiped out all of the potato crop one year. They had become so dependent on spuds, that to survive they had to emigrate to America. We all know the consequences that the tobacco plant brought with it. Fortunately Sir Walter got his just deserts by being incarcerated in the Tower of London for a number of years,

Even as I write this, I have just received the sad news of the death of my great friend Ron. Smoking was the root cause of his death. I hope anyone reading this and who is addicted to smoking will endeavour to do as I did. (KICK IT.)

We lads 'the Fearless Four' got bored one time during the summer school holiday and decided to go on an adventure. We decided to go camping down by the riverside at Chertsey. Lionel owned a small ridge tent and also his two older sisters owned girls' sit-up-and-beg bicycles, i.e. upright bikes with skirt protectors over the rear wheels. We made a slight modification to them by changing the rear wheel retaining nuts to elongated ones. Behind the saddle we fitted a carrier on which to sit; having loaded the front basket with a few supplies, we set off taking it in turns to do the peddling. Eventually we arrived at our destination. The first thing to do was to pitch the tent. Next was to gather wood for our fire. This was in abundance – driftwood from the banks of the river supplemented by fallen branches from nearby trees. The first day went by like magic, what with swimming – having passed our tests by now – and climbing the trees. No need to pass a test for that. After knocking up some sort of meal, we got our heads down and slept like logs.

The next morning, after a dip in the Thames, we were starving. Two of us needed to go into the local village to get bread and a couple of pounds of bangers and a dozen eggs. That was about all the money we had. Later that day, it was time to return home. Our mums would start to worry if we tried to stay longer. After dismantling the tent and cleaning up, to our horror we discovered a puncture in the front wheel of one of our bikes. Having forgotten to bring a puncture repair outfit with us and not having any money left, we stuffed the tyre with straw and grass, with more in reserve, and headed for home undaunted, still in good spirits.

What shall we talk about now? I know – trams. Not the horse-drawn ones of mother's day but the electric ones of my school days (1926–1936). You know, the ones that we used to curse whenever our bicycle wheels got stuck in the rails. These rails, incidentally, were covered in when trolley buses came on the scene. Later when there was a shortage of steel, it was lucrative to dig the rails up, cut them up and cart them away. A mate of mine was employed for this job, with an acetylene gas torch. While digging up the rails, wooden tar blocks were exposed, many of which somehow found their way into our kitchen fires. They burnt brilliantly; the only snag was the occasional bang when a piece of grit or flint exploded.

Whilst on the subject of the household fire, the chimney had to be cleaned now and then. The sweeper would come around and it was our job to let him know when his brushes came out of the chimney top. If you could not afford to pay a chimney sweep, the dodge was to send a ball of lighted paper up the said chimney thus setting fire to the soot. If perchance this got out of hand, the fire brigade did not appreciate a call out. Sometimes this was done accidentally, as we were in the habit of holding a piece of newspaper in front of the fire to create a draft to draw up the fire. If you were not careful, this would catch alight and be sucked up the chimney. Never a dull moment in those days. In the advent of our district being made into a smokeless zone, it was frowned on to make use of these methods. No wonder we used to have peasouper fogs in the days before smokeless zones.

On the subject of trams, I never envied the tram driver. He had to stand up on his platform which was open to all of the elements, rain, snow or fog. His only protection was a pair of heavy duty goggles, a waterproof hat and an oilskin raincoat. The only advantage over a bus driver was in foggy weather because the rails kept him on the straight and narrow. Passengers on the upper deck had no protection at all, as there was no roof to the tram or bus. By the way, a tram could be driven from the front or the rear. This was handy for the return journeys. Just change over the overhead connection rods to the overhead electric lines. The passenger seats were reversible. The one advantage of riding upstairs in rainy weather for a bus passenger was that in front of you was a waterproof cover you could unroll and place over your knees. Buses during foggy days were led along by a man with a flaming torch.

At this time of year there is another event, namely the burning of the effigy of the notorious Guy Fawkes. Most of us enjoy the occasion on 5th November. When we were young kids, the thing was to make all these effigies by stuffing a sack filled with fallen leaves for the main torso. Make a head with a bag of old rags, put a mask on it and plonk an old hat on top and lo and behold we had a Guy. Sit it in an old handmade box cart, plonk it outside a shop and use an old can for a begging bowl and we were in business. All very fine until a tragic accident. One of these Guys was placed outside a butchers shop. The butcher came out and playfully stabbed it with his knife. Unfortunately, he never realised that this particular Guy was a small kid dressed up. It was rumoured that the boy had died, but everything was quickly hushed up, as it was bad for business. What a sad day all round – it certainly dampened the event that year.

I can recall my first trip to the seaside. This is what happened. Very near to where we lived is an off-licence, selling wines and spirits. Now this particular one was owned by a very kindly old lady. My friend and I used to deliver the various pamphlets for her business to the houses. For our efforts, she offered to take us to Southend-on-Sea for the day. As we were only about eleven years old, permission had to be granted by our parents. You can imagine the excitement when this was granted. We were agog at our first glimpse of the sea. What with buying the seaside rock – with Southend-on-Sea lettered all the way through it – and ice cream and lemonade, we were in dreamland. A good dinner of fish and chips went down well. We sampled cockles and shrimps. All of it was wonderful and something I shall never forget.

The only way poor people could get a holiday away from home was a working holiday, hop picking. The whole family would transport themselves in a lorry to the hop fields in Kent. The farmers would provide sheds for their living accommodation. The workers had a thoroughly good time when the day's work was done. They booked up for this every year.

Unfortunately, I never had this opportunity. Nevertheless, we had plenty of scope for enjoyment locally, namely, all the places to visit aforementioned. Hop picking is now done mechanically.

My first job after leaving school at the age of fourteen was a job in a printing firm. I lasted only two weeks there as the randy girls kept grabbing my privates. The next job was more to my liking, working in an entire man's world. I was made more or less the tea boy and grease monkey. I didn't mind that, you have to start at the bottom and work your way up the ladder. This was the start of my engineering career in this garage in Richmond. The men were quite friendly and introduced me to men's pastimes such as watching all-in wrestling in the Coronation Hall. Another thing was the dirt track riding at Wembley. After a couple of enjoyable years with them, I was offered another garage job in a small garage in Richmond, next to the ice drome, paying me more money. A great step up the ladder to fame and fortune – ha ha.

The owner of this garage was a very good man who taught me a lot about garage work and engineering. He had some sort of connection with the ice drome. He invented the first plough to be used for skimming the surface of the ice after it was damaged by the skaters. This was quite an achievement. Prior to that, the process was to spray water over the ice and have to waste considerable time re-freezing the surface. What we did together, the boss and I, was to cut down the chassis of a bull-nosed Morris car and turn it into a tractor to pull the said plough over the ice. For a cutting edge we obtained an eight-foot guillotine blade from a local publishing company. This plough was so successful that we were commissioned to manufacture similar ones for Wembley and Haringey Ice Rinks. I earned a nice bit of pocket money attending to the rink's car park on the days when the Richmond Ice Hockey Team were playing at home and for other events such as Figure Skating Championships. Celia College was our champ.

Another event was a barrel-jumping contest. Red McCarthy boasted at being the person with the most broken bones on the way to being World Champ. Now Red used to have his SS100 sports car serviced by me in our garage. When he was finished, he used to take me for a spin. He was just as mad in the car as he was on the ice. I was lucky because Raymond, the boss's son, and I went to all the ice hockey matches for free. I went in for speed skating and ended up in the first-aid room with a suspected broken nose, with blood pouring down my new trousers – you can imagine the mess. I was soaked to the skin with the mixture of ice, slush and blood.

When I joined the Royal Air Force in 1938, I pawned my ice hockey skates at Uncles, the pawnshop in Richmond. Where I was going I would not be needing them. My boss was a retired Royal Flying Corps officer. It was through his good offices that I was able to enlist into the Royal Air Force.

The RAF were very choosy in those days as to who they allowed into their ranks. After a stiff entrance exam, both physical and mental, I was honoured and allowed to enlist for a term of six years with the colours and six years in the reserve. Right up to the outbreak of the Second World War, Britain was going through a period of disarmament for economic reasons to recover from the aftermath of the World War I slump. The armed forces were being reduced considerably in numbers and naval pay slashed by 50 per cent.

Whilst memories are flooding back, I recall making a crystal set to receive radio broadcasts. This consisted of a board upon which was mounted a clamp to hold a small piece of crystal, opposite this was a device called a cat's whisker. After a lot of fiddling about you could get a signal from the station you were tuned into. Apart from London, you could get Radio Athlone, Radio Normandy and Radio

Luxemburg. The aerial I rigged up in my bedroom was yards and yards of copper wire that I had unwound from a scrapped magneto and strung around the room next to the ceiling. A pair of headphones completed the whole outfit. Having no electricity installed in our house, the wireless set was battery and accumulator operated which had to be periodically charged. Our house was illuminated by gaslight, oil lamp and candles. The gas lamp filament was so fragile, it was often damaged at lighting up times.

Exit Ernie Junior – welcome to Ernie Senior.

Part Two

At War and After

ON THE 23 October 1938, when I was seventeen and a quarter years of age, I was privileged to be allowed to join the ranks of the illustrious Royal Air Force, formerly the Royal Flying Corps. After accepting the King's Shilling and swearing allegiance to King and Country at Victory House, we were transported to RAF Uxbridge for preliminary training. First of all, the King's Shilling lasted us about an hour. We were marched to the station's camp barber for a haircut; this was despite the fact that prior to enlisting, I had my hair trimmed in civvy street. When I voiced my objection, I was threatened with being charged with insubordination. Good start!

After paying the barber for a skinhead haircut, we were taken to the NAAFI, meaning Navy, Army and Air Force Institute, to purchase boot polish and metal polish. This left us with tuppence which we 'voluntarily' donated to the Royal Air Force Benevolent Fund. Whilst we were at Uxbridge, we were taught how to make up and dismantle a 'Macdonald's bed'. This consisted of a metal bedstead which could be converted to a chair. The mattress was made up with 'three biscuits'. Everything had to be done perfectly as demonstrated. The next place to visit was the Stores to get kitted out, making sure the boots had the regulation number of studs embedded in the soles. This was essential because this was one of the things always looked for on numerous kit inspections. One thing I loathed was the military cap called the 'Glengarry'. The only way to stop the damned thing from falling off was to hold your head at a permanent angle.

They kitted us out very well. We had two tunics (one was for everyday use and one for ceremonial occasions. The ordinary one was called a 'dog collar'). Two trousers complete with braces. Two shirts, two vests, two pants, two pairs of socks. Four brushes, one of which was a shaving brush, although some of us had not started to shave yet, one button brush for all the brass, one clothes brush and one boot brush. One button stick, one holdall and one 'house-wife' complete with needles, cotton and spare buttons and a roll of darning wool. All this had to be accounted for on every kit inspection. This had to be all paid for out of our Clothing Allowance, which we had in peace time, to be done away with when war broke out in 1939. Our first night sleeping away from home was embarrassing for me: I could hear sobbing coming from one or two beds being occupied by 'Mother's Darling Boys'. Grow up; you are in the Forces now! You are not a person now, you are a number, mine being 627311. This it was well for you to remember, as you could not receive your weekly pay without stating your service number and saluting 'sir'.

From Uxbridge, we were assigned to Henlow RAF station, or to RAF Debden in Essex. This was the station I was allotted to. They even had aircraft there. After being put through the mill with drill instructors trying to break our spirits with all the square bashing and rifle practice with bayonet, lobbing a grenade, Sten gun firing and having to strip and assemble the Lewis Gun blindfold, we were ready for our passing-out parade. Not all of us survived this ordeal and, being peacetime, parents were allowed to buy out their lovely boys who could not stay the pace.

We had one particularly sadistic PTI (Physical Training Instructor): his request for a Weekend Pass was turned down, so he took his spite out on us. He had us doubling up and down on the parade ground until one of us collapsed from sheer fatigue. Now, I am quite prepared to accept discipline, but this was well out of order. That night after I had downed a couple of pints in the NAAFI, I decided a bit of rough justice was called for. This Corporal Instructor was in the habit of parking his motorcycle near to the NAAFI and whilst my mate kept 'doggo', I proceeded to top up the instructor's petrol tank with Ernie High Octane, free of charge. I walked away quite relieved. I don't think he got very far on this type of fuel. I think he got the message because it was noticeable that he behaved more reasonably in future.

One way of giving us an appetite for breakfast was to make us run around the perimeter of the aerodrome. One day we heard a terrific bang. Apparently a Hurricane fighter plane had failed to pull out of a power dive. When we got to the crash site, the only piece of the 'kite' sticking out of the ground was the tail plane. The pilot's body had become mangled up with the engine.

After they had taught us discipline and turned us out in prime physical condition, we were posted to either RAF Cardington where, incidentally, the Airship R101 was housed, or RAF Manston, which is situated between Margate and Ramsgate. I was quite happy to be posted to RAF Manston and to be taught basic engineering skills. Apart from being located in this lovely area, the only thing that comes to mind is this:

Upon arrival at this station, we were allocated to a hut

with its usual number of beds and bed space. After we had settled in, we had the inevitable kit layout for inspection. Unfortunately, my bed was directly under a window which had a pane of glass broken. Upon inspection I was charged for the broken pane, plus the replacement and to add to the insult, had to pay for the one to go back into the stores. What a racket!

At the end of this training, there were the usual examinations. Those above a certain percentage were to be funnelled into the higher grade, i.e. the best Flight Mechanics were promoted to become Aero Engine Fitters; this included me. The rest were to become Flight Riggers and Airframe Fitters. RAF St Athan was our next posting. Whilst at this station, war was declared and we spent some time filling up sandbags. We settled down after a couple of false air raid alarms. After an intense period of engineering training, we were split up and posted to various squadrons; I joined No. 78 Bomber Squadron to work on Whitney Bombers at Dishforth in Yorkshire, and afterwards at Linton-on-Ouse. Our first air raids over Germany were leaflet raids: propaganda pamphlets pointing out to the German people all the monies stashed abroad in the names of Hitler and his fellow henchmen. All our aircraft returned safely, the main reason being that our aircraft were well into the return journey by the time that the leaflets fluttered to the ground.

When this operation proved ineffective, we switched to using bombs. Not all the leaflets landed on Germany. Quite a few came home to us because upon landing, some leaflets that had been trapped behind the bomb doors were released when the Bungy sprung doors opened on impact. My mates and I retrieved quite a few.

Our flight was posted temporarily to a makeshift landing place on the farmland near Banbury, Oxfordshire. We had to rough it, but we didn't mind that as there was a special job to be undertaken. We slept in a cow shed on palliasses filled with straw and our water came in a cleaned out petrol bowser. We were issued with flying boats and sweaters and excused from shaving. Once a week, we flew to the nearest RAF station for a bath and a shave. This station was a proper 'spit and polish' one and they had a fit when they saw us scruffs land on their immaculate drome. They threatened to put us on a charge but soon backed down when our Flight Commander whispered in their ear.

When we returned to snowbound Yorkshire, the rest of our squadron were jealous to see us slightly sunburned from the 'sunny South!' One particularly bitterly cold day whilst on the mainplane of my kite, filling up the fuel tanks from the 'bowser', my hands got frozen to the nozzle release trigger and the High Octane flooded all over the mainplane. My mate had to switch off the pump in the bowser and release me. Our aircraft were at Dispersal alongside of the Great North Road. They had to be picketed down facing the wind. These pickets were bloody great corkscrews six feet long, which had to be screwed into the frozen ground. The planes were then lashed down with ropes at special points. If the wind happened to change direction, we had to manhandle them to face the wind and reposition the aforesaid pickets, exercise which kept us from freezing to death.

At that time (1939–1940) the IRA was rearing its ugly head, consequently we had to do aircraft protection guard patrol. This was over and above our normal maintenance duties, all in a day's work. I was not sorry to be posted to a secret destination on my own. Secrecy was drummed into us in those dire days when our ships were suffering heavy losses. I was ordered to report to the admin office where I was shown a map of the world. The officer's finger pointed to a place called Rhodesia. I had a rough idea where it was, as I was pretty good at geography at school. I was told to go to the Stores and get kitted out with tropical gear, i.e. Wolesley sun helmet and khaki drill clothing, etc. From there, off to the Medical Officer for numerous jabs in the buttocks against all the known tropical diseases.

With a travel warrant, I was told to proceed to RAF Uxbridge and report my presence. Whilst at this base, I met up with a few of my mates from other stations. We spent two nights 'under canvas', meaning tents. From there we entrained to Southampton where the large ship, *The Arundel Castle* was waiting to take us to Cape Town in South Africa. As our train approached Southampton and was pulling slowly into the station, the locals asked if they could post our last-minute letters for us. Very kind indeed. They told us that the day previously the docks had been heavily bombed. We lost no time in getting underway, before the Germans concentrated their heavy bombing of docks. The main targets were airfields.

It was becoming too dangerous to carry on training pilots in Britain so it was decided to open up training bases in Canada and Rhodesia. Our lot were on the way to open up several bases surrounding Salisbury, the capital of Southern Rhodesia, later to be renamed Harare Zimbabwe. Our ship, *The Arundel Castle*, was a very fast boat. So we were allowed to proceed unescorted instead of taking our place in a convoy. Our armament was one four-inch gun forward and one four-inch gun aft, manned by a few Marines. Fortunately for us, our ship had not been converted to a troop ship. We had bunks to sleep on, not like the ones I have been on since; in these ones we were issued with ham-mocks.[1] Of a night time we would go up on deck and watch the wake of our ship, this was quite pretty to see, because of

---

[1] *The Arundel Castle* still had normal sleeping accommodation (bunk beds) for civilian use. When large ships were commandeered for troop carrying, bunk beds were removed to make more room. Troops were issued with a hammock apiece, to sling as per navy fashion. See also p.50.

all the phosphorescence churned up. You could see the zigzag pattern; we had to continuously change course (hard to port for a short period, then hard to starboard) to avoid enemy torpedoes.

We had amazing luck on the outward journey. When we put into Dakar for oil and water, the French Battleship *Richelieu* was in the harbour, it being a French base off West Africa, close to the equator. We airmen went up on deck and gave the French sailors the traditional salute of two fingers. They did not appreciate this friendly gesture. They turned their bloody great guns on us. However, this is the hairy bit. We mistimed our visit because in 1940 the French capitulated to the Germans, having been outmanoeuvred and pushed into the sea at Dunkirk, our expeditionary force with them. When we put into port for oil and water, a cutter came out to us to warn the captain to leave sharpish, as the Vichy French were about to take over. This we did with no hesitation, not wanting to be interned for the duration of the hostilities. These brave British agents saved us from years of misery in this hellhole named White Man's Graveyard.

The next day when we were well underway, the captain of our ship spoke to us over the Tannoy system informing us that our agents had blown up the stern of the aforementioned Battleship *Richelieu*. This put her out of action for six months, otherwise she would have been on our tail.

It was quite noticeable at night watching our wake that we were making a beeline towards Cape Town instead of zigzagging. All this necessitated our being rationed for water. You can imagine the unclean, unshaven state of us upon arrival. We were given salt-water soap when we took a salt-water shower. This was bloody useless leaving us in a sticky mess. However, we just about made it to our friendly port. Future British shipping refuelled at Freetown a little further down the coast.

Other things come to mind, like watching schools of porpoises playing around in the sea. There were flying fish and so-called Spanish Galleon. Later during the war, the Vichy Navy was given the option of either proceeding to a neutral port or surrendering to the Royal Navy. They did neither, so the Royal Navy subsequently sunk them. All's well that ends well.

After the First World War, (in which my uncle was killed at the age of seventeen years – he had falsified his age to enlist; my father suffered lung trouble after a gas attack) the Allies went through the depression years. In order to economise, the Government thought it a good idea to remove our occupying Army from being stationed along the river Rhine, against French advice. Very bad mistake, almost fatal.

Our planners, who could not plan a piss-up in a brewery, staked all our future in the Maginot Line, a supposedly impregnable defence line facing the Germans. Anyone with half an eye could spot the glaringly obvious weak link. The line finished at the Belgium border. Naturally the German Army were not stupid enough to bang their heads against this impregnable line. Simply, slip around the end of the line, through Belgium and into France that way. Which was exactly what they did. So all the years of suffering the British people had had to endure was down to these prats.

During the period before the Second World War, Britain was disarming for economic reasons. A false economy, because the Germans were rearming and determined to disregard the Armistice terms and conditions. They were going to have another bang at us. Our Prime Minister, Neville Chamberlain went to see Hitler and did a deal with him. Hitler signed a sort of non-aggression pact and in return we more or less sacrificed the nation of Czechoslovakia to Germany. This gave us about a year's reprieve. We used this time to pull our fingers out and prepare ourselves to face the inevitable onslaught that was to come.

Now let us get back to the business of pursuing the progress of war. Upon arrival at Simonstown, the Naval Base of Cape Town, we entrained for the journey to Southern Rhodesia. Being at sea level, it is necessary to climb up to the top of the plateau which is named Table Mountain. To enable us to do this, two strong railway engines slowly wind their way to the top. Now we were in for a three day journey to our destination. The most memorable stop we made was at Mafeking, the place that Baden-Powell and his troops were relieved from the siege. The best part of the town came out to fete us as we were the first troops to visit them since the siege.

We stopped now and again to gather firewood to supplement the coal-fired boilers of the train engine. The train driver used to pull up now and again for us to stretch our legs. He took advantage of this to bring out his rifle and shoot a steinbuck. This was a bit tough to eat, but a change from the usual fare. We changed trains at Bulawayo, and then on to the capital city of Salisbury. It did not take us long to get stuck in and get on with the job we were sent out to do, namely train 'sprogs', as we called them, into pilots.

The EFTS (Elementary Flight Training School) was based at Belvedere. I was based at Cranbourne to serve in the IFTS (Intermediary Flying Training School). The EFTS used Tiger Moth Aircraft with a fixed undercarriage. The sprogs, after learning the elementaries of flying, were sent to us to be turned into pilots and get their 'wings'.

One of the very few features of the monotonous journey from the Cape to Salisbury and which relieved the boredom was the sight of thousands upon thousands of termite mounds. These mounds look like a forest of trees that had been cut down to about eight feet. One more thing I can recall is the sight of huge rock formations. Some of these are miraculously balanced one on top of another. They are so finely balanced that they rock in the wind but never fall off.

We had a wonderful welcome in Salisbury. The white population at the time was only 10,000. Perhaps the fact that they were outnumbered by about a hundred to one by the native population had a bearing on this. Maybe I'm a bit cynical. They were practically lining up to have the privilege of inviting us to their homes. Bless them. I expect they were eager to learn of the news from home; most of them had roots in the United Kingdom. Four of us likely lads soon made friends with a Mr Scott who happened to own the Flowing Bowl Gold Mine. We spent quite a few weekends being invited to mix with his family. I must say they did us proud. I remember volunteering to turn the sheet music over whilst one of his daughters played beautifully at the grand piano. My mates were a bit jealous because I could read music and they couldn't. At one time Mr Scott was considering adopting us because he had no sons.

This is how we first met up with Mr Scott. Three other erks and myself clubbed together and bought a clapped out old Chevey car. We went out and about to see what the country had to offer us. Well sure enough, one day when we were in the middle of nowhere in particular, our luck ran out. Our jalopy broke down. Fortunately, we were not too far off the beaten track, where we thumbed a lift. The first car to draw up was a small one that could not accommodate four extra persons, so we decided to stick together and declined the offer of two seats. Fortunately Mr Scott appeared on the scene, like a knight in shinning armour and rescued us from our plight. Hence the friendship and subsequent visits to his extensive property. We had a guided tour of his gold mine and holdings. Natives were only allowed in town with a work permit and had to get off the footpath at the approach of a white person. When accepting anything from a white person, it had to be taken with both hands extended. Apparently this was for safety reasons. There was a nightly curfew for them. White colonists had to maintain severe rules to keep superiority over them.

One day my medical officer sent me to Salisbury General Hospital to 'volunteer' a blood donation. Apparently my blood group was urgently needed and in short supply. After giving them an armful of blood they practically begged me for more. Me being of a generous nature agreed. It must have been about one hundred percent alcohol. In exchange they gave me a couple of cups of sweet tea. After resting for a while, I was wending my weary way back to camp when a Rolls Royce car with liveried driver pulled up alongside and a lady's voice came from the rear seat asking if I would like to have a lift. The driver opened the rear door and allowed me to be seated beside the lady. We were soon in deep conversation. Apparently she had two sons serving with the Royal Air Force in England. It turned out that she was about the richest woman in Salisbury. Her husband owned about the best part of the city including Meikles Hotel and the swank Meikles department store. She said she had come into town to keep an appointment with her hairdresser. After her taking leave of me, she gave instructions to the chauffeur that he and the car were at my disposal for as long as I desired. Naturally, it took me a very very long time to return to my camp, not a bad day out. The driver informed me the Meikles owned ten luxurious cars.

One of the important duties of a flight mechanic was to give the sprog pilots their cockpit drill. This could be very frustrating at times, especially when they failed to start the engine first time. The only thing that made it bearable was the fact they did not have rank whilst under training and we spoke to them in good old-fashioned English, if you know what I mean. Quite a lot of them were Polish and some were Greek with names like Didmontropolis or Popapopov. We quickly renamed them as Dick, Tom and Harry or some not quite so complimentary name. The way to start up the Wasp Engine of our Harvard Planes was by winding up the so-called Inertia Starter. After winding your guts out, this had to be quickly engaged to the engine. If it failed to start first time, the process had to be repeated. It being quite hot in Rhodesia, you can imagine it was not Polish or Greek that was spoken.

Quite often when I was on night-flying duty, one of my flying instructors would come out of the mess slightly inebriated and I had to practically lift him into the cockpit and strap him in. It was amazing how quickly he sobered up once he got airborne. The main training at night was what is called circuits and bumps, i.e. circling the drome and landing. For safety, we used an Aldis lamp to control the several planes in circuit at the same time. An Aldis lamp shines quite a bright light; this could be green or red denoting whether or not the pilot had permission to land or to make another circuit. The lamp had sights on it which could be aimed at the pilot. Now my wayward instructor sometimes cut corners to jump the queue and land so that he could get back to the mess and finish what he had started, namely to get pissed. I, being in a jocular mood, would give him a red light to make him circuit once again. There was plenty of fist-shaking when I eventually allowed him to land.

At night time when we switched the 'chance light' on it attracted enormous moths as lights do. We used to arm ourselves with a stick when we were dive bombed by them. It was not only moths that attacked us, there were beetles the size of tortoises that got into the act. However, that was what we were being paid for. The 'chance light' was like a searchlight that was directed along the ground by the 'Flare Path' so that a pilot could land safely at night.

The personnel of the Rhodesian Air Force intermingled very well with the RAF. One of them was Ian Smith who was later to become Prime Minister of Rhodesia. One of his mates was Chummy Paige, a corporal who worked with us on our planes.

One day a native was riding round the perimeter on a bicycle; an Oxford Plane came in to land and the leading edge of the mainplane decapitated him. We had the job of cleaning up the mess and repairing the damage.

Another tasty job was to retrieve a plane that had landed in the town's sewerage farm. We had a couple of dozen natives with ropes to haul it out. Fortunately, the pilot was still alive and he had to pay a forfeit. We had a scheme whereby the sprog pilots donated a certain amount of cash to the celebration booze-up when they received their wings. There were fixed fines: so much for a wing tip replacement dug into the ground whilst landing; another was when they forgot to lower the undercarriage upon landing and did a belly flop. This happened quite frequently because they had recently been flying Tiger Moths that had a fixed undercart. Sometimes they ended up with their tails in the air because they applied the brakes too early. A complete write off was the most expensive fine.

We flight mechanics and riggers were allocated two Harvard Trainers apiece to maintain. I, being in charge of the Commanding Officer's plane, took my place at the end of a line of planes as we did the warm-up of our engines, well before the pilots came on the scene. Now, the Commanding Officer was the only one who had his wife living with him on the camp. The other wives were shipped out to us months afterwards. To make sure he had an early morning call, I made a certain signal by raising my arm through the cockpit canopy so that we could all synchronise our full throttle procedure and change the propeller pitch. The racket that was produced was enough to raise the dead.

You would have thought he would appreciate this, but he showed no approving gesture.

We had a very nasty, ignorant warrant officer – a disciplinarian. Whilst conducting a party of civilians around the planes, he was overheard saying to them, 'wonderful planes these, all iron... and this is the starting handle,' pointing to the pilot head, a device to register airspeed. One day whilst returning from a train journey to the Victoria Falls, he was accidentally pushed off the train. Luckily for him the train was not going too fast and he survived.

From the laminated blade of a wooden propeller, I made a novelty pop-up cigarette case. I would show off my case by sliding the lid along and proffering a cigarette to an acquaintance. A very light spring made the cigarette pop up for reception.

In our hut we had a 'house boy' to keep the place clean, also he would do the dhobi and ironing of our khaki drill. 'House boy'! he was old enough to be our father. I had great sympathy for him because he had elephantiasis – a horrible infliction whereby one leg was as thick as an elephant's. In our billet we had mosquito nets over beds and a couple of chameleons to combat the mosquitoes. Some hope!

One weekend I managed to contract malaria. The medical officer was away, as usual, and I had a raging fever. My mates covered me with their blankets to get the fever down, although with malaria you get the shivers and feel cold. They boiled up some lemon and made me sweat it out. It worked out OK. That's why I'm alive to write this story. As you never quite get malaria out of your system, I have had a few attacks since in 'civvy street' – very nasty.

Another incident comes to mind. One morning when I was orderly corporal, the night guard woke me up with the usual mug of tea and a signature from me to prove this. Unfortunately for me, I dropped off to sleep again. Anyway,

Ernie's mum with Timmy (Pete's Son), 1959

Ernie at his bench

Cranbourn Camp, Southern Rhodesia

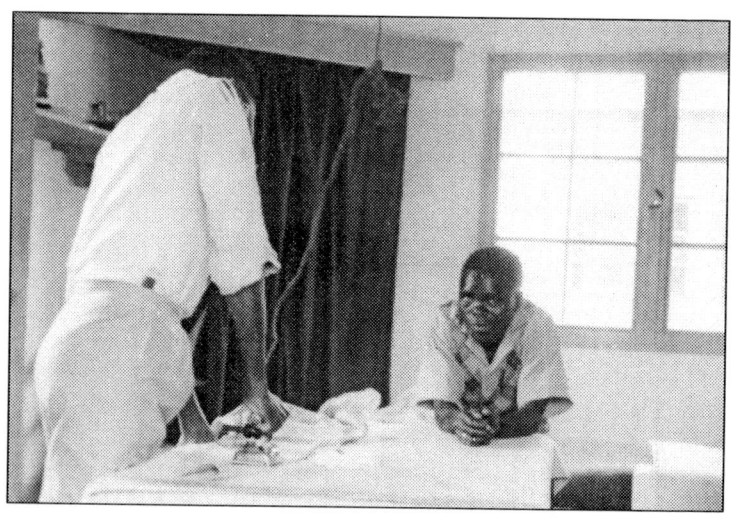

The 'house boy', showing signs of elephantiasis

Larking about when off duty

Ernie' mates and mascot outside their hut

A native postman

A view of outside Cranbourn Camp

A forest fire

A typical railway station in Africa

Bulawayo Railway station, 1940

Chummy Paige sticking his head out of the train window

Chummy Paige

Locusts approach the airfield

Cloud of locusts

Walking among native areas

Salisbury, the capital of Southern Rhodesia

Giraffe at camp boundary fence

Zebra at camp boundary fence

Okapi

Warthog

Warthog

Gazelles or antelopes

Zebra

Railway bridge astride the Zambezi River near Victoria Falls

A closer view

Victoria Falls

Part of the Falls

Looking up at Victoria Falls

Zambezi River

Zambezi River

Zambezi River

Inline engines

Radial engine

Our liberator bomber at Kinley Field, Bermuda

Work outing – Brentford Gas Works

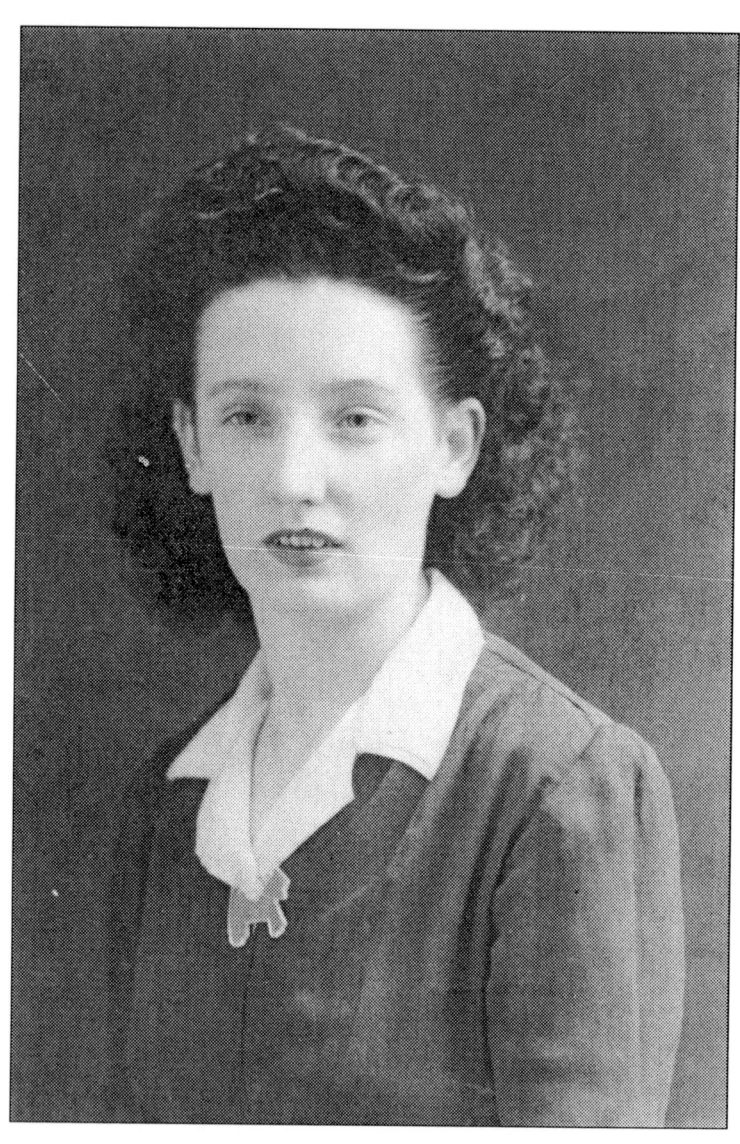

Ernie's wife, Vera

Ernie in his demob suit with his wife Vera, 1947

NORTH THAMES GAS BOARD

30 KENSINGTON CHURCH STREET W.8
Telegrams : Coalgas Kens London
Telephone : WEStern 8141

22nd August, 1949.

Dear Mr. Hoare,

I am pleased to say that the
Board have accepted the recommendation of
the Awards Committee that you should
receive an award for your suggestion
for -

A fabricated tool for riveting clutch
linings on Dennis "Ace" vehicles.

They have therefore voted
you Ten guineas in appreciation of that
suggestion.

The Board hope that there may
be other occasions on which they will
have the pleasure of rewarding you in
this way.

Yours faithfully,

Secretary.

Mr. E.V. Hoare,
Motor Repairer,
Brentford.

my mates rallied round me and got the planes pushed out of the hangar and warmed up for the day's flying as quickly as possible. My squadron leader appreciated the effort put in and only sentenced me to seven days confined to camp. It could have been far worse.

The mornings were bitterly cold owing to the altitude, Rhodesia being on a plateau of 6,000 feet. On top of our tropical khaki we put on our Air Force blue. This we discarded when the temperature rose. By the time we went in for breakfast, we were down to bush shirt and shorts. Sometimes during the rainy season, the water flowed off the airfield in such abundance as to fill up the gullies which surrounded the field for that purpose. In a very short time these gullies were filled with rainwater. This enabled us to swim back to the cookhouse for breakfast.

Believe it or not the dry season gets a bit boring weather-wise. This lasts about ten months, with not a cloud to be seen in the sky to put a pattern on the bright blue heavens. One day we did not believe our eyes. On the horizon was a big black cloud approaching us. However, this was not a rain cloud, but a cloud of locusts. Millions upon millions of them. Locusts are like flying grasshoppers, only these are big as cigars. They descended upon us and for miles around consumed every bit of vegetation in sight. Some landed on trees, the branches of which could not withstand the sheer weight, so that they snapped off. Now some of our aircraft were getting low on fuel and had to land among them. When they landed and taxied to a standstill, the air-cooled engines were smothered with locusts frying away merrily on the red-hot engines. The natives we had working for us could hardly wait until the propellers stopped rotating to get at this feast of delicacies. They would tear off the head and wings and get stuck in. Not much different from shrimps or prawns. At least locusts don't feed off dead bodies. Many a farmer has been ruined by this pest eating all their crops, whether of maize or tobacco.

Another boring job was 'drogue towing'. A drogue was similar to a wind sock placed at a corner of an airfield which indicated wind direction, needed by the pilots to head into wind for take offs or landings. The Harvard Trainer was dual controlled, with a sprog pilot in the front cockpit with dashboard instruments and controls. The fully trained instructor was in the rear cockpit with dual control. I went up in the sprog's seat, mainly for ballast. We took off dragging the drogue behind us on a long cable. Once we were airborne and reached the desired altitude, we proceeded to the firing range which was located along the Mazoe Dam, three and a half miles long. The occupants of the pursuing aircraft would fire at the drogue we were towing at a safe distance. After a time of flying up and down above the dam my pilot got bored stiff and got me to do this chore for him while he could read a novel in the rear cockpit. This was nothing to it, just keep your eye on the altitude, etc. and you soon got used to the controls for banking and steering. The pilot, needless to say, kept his eye on his mate Ernie. After about three hours of this monotonous operation, we came in to land having released the drogue directly we were over our airfield.

In Rhodesia the sun rises very quickly at about 6 a.m. and sets just as quickly at about 6 p.m. One morning at about sunrise, I had warmed up the engine of my first plane, strapped the pilot and his sprog in their seats and sent them on their way for the take off. Soon afterwards I did likewise for my second plane. My rigger and I proceeded to the flight hut to sign the required Form 700 as usual, when we heard a terrific bang behind us. We stood transfixed for a second and rushed to the scene of the crash. To our horror, one plane was upside down with a wing torn off and aircraft fuel gushing out in gallons. All we knew was we had to get the occupants out at the double in case the lot went up in flames. The occupants were hanging upside down in their harnesses. We managed to get the one in the rear cockpit out very quickly, but the one in the front cockpit had his foot trapped under the rudder bar. I got my hacksaw out of my toolbox sharpish and said to the sprog, 'Don't worry, I'm sawing it off.' With that, he fainted. When we eventually got him out he said that he thought that I was going to cut his foot off. What had happened was that the pilot had been blinded by the sun in his eyes just as he was airborne and did not see the plane that was taxing below him. After we had all given evidence at the Court of Inquiry, it ended with an accidental verdict. If there had not been a crash pylon between the two cockpits, the pilots would not have survived.

The reason why I joined the RAF in the first place was to eventually get my wings and return to civvy street and be an airline pilot. The best laid plans of mice and men and all that fits my case perfectly. Along came the war and my plans were sunk without a trace. Nevertheless I tried another way and kept applying for pilot training. I was told to stop pestering and get on with the work I was paid to do, the reason being that a lot of time and money had been spent on me to become a technician and that we were turning out pilots within six weeks training.

It took a long time before any of us got a decent leave period. My erstwhile Irish friend and I decided to go to Johannesburg. We chose the wrong time to go because while we were there it snowed. In living memory, nobody had ever seen snow there. My mate and I were not dressed for the occasion, as we assumed khaki bush shirt and shorts would be adequate. We made do with confining ourselves to hotels and pubs. Then it warmed up and a good time was enjoyed by us. Unfortunately, this was why we missed our train to return to camp in Southern Rhodesia.

We were now up the proverbial creek without a paddle. What to do next. At the railway station we were told the earliest time to book the very long train journey to Salisbury, Rhodesia was ten days. This we failed to do. Might as well get hung for a sheep as for a lamb or whatever the saying is.

All in all we were arrested and charged upon arrival at camp with being absent without leave for twenty days and six hours. When I was marched in front or our commanding officer to give my account as to why I was adrift, I recited a cock and bull story we had rehearsed together, my mate and I. After listening to my tale of woe, my commanding officer commended me with my efforts to return to duty, and asked me whether I would accept his punishment or opt for a court martial. Knowing the maximum punishment he could dish out to me with his rank was fourteen days' jankers, I accepted his punishment of ten days' jankers and twenty-one days' pay stopped. When I was marched out and passed my pal on the way in, I whispered to him, 'Accept it.' Now all we had to do was to sweat it out at the double for ten days in full pack drill and to lay out our kit every hour in the guard room. We soon sweated out all the beer we had drunk in Johannesburg.

Whilst in Jo'burg, we considered joining the South African Air Force because they were paying more money than the RAF. They did not want to get involved. A long time after this my misdeeds would catch up with me, because when my group came up for demobilisation, I had to remain behind for twenty-one days to complete the AWOL.

It was still a bit primitive in those days. On the outskirts of town was a public bar we would visit to knock back a pint or two. On the outside was a hitching rail for the gold prospectors to tie up their horses. On the bar inside was a pair of scales for them to weigh their poke of gold. Most often they would stay in residence until their dosh ran out, then it was back to doing a bit more prospecting.

We taught some of the natives to play football. They became quite good players and could kick a ball barefooted from one end of the pitch to the far end. Whilst on guard duty we were expected to go out on patrol regardless of the heat, but the native Askari Guards were provided with a 'pill box' for shelter from the sun. Talk about mad dogs and Englishmen going out in the midday sun! Good job we had the efficient Wolesley helmet to protect us from the relentless sun.

One night whilst taking a short cut through the woods from the Married Quarters Social Club back to camp, I had quite a shock. In the darkness I heard a loud hissing sound, expecting to be confronted by a snake, I was relieved to see the outline of a native on a bicycle who had applied his brakes to avoid hitting me, hence the hissing sound. In future I took the long way round back to camp.

I got quite friendly with a corporal's wife, if you know what I mean. She was quite blatant in showing her feelings for me. There were plenty of tears when it came time for me to be repatriated back to England.

After a three and a half year tour of duty some of us embarked upon the P&O *SS Stratheden* to return to the UK. This journey took six weeks, whereas the outward journey took only the ten days that I have previously written about.

Not all of us returned because some had married Rhodesian girls. I was pleased to return before my affair with the Corporal's wife got out of hand. Prior to our embarkation, we had to spend about a week or so at 'Camp Retreat', an RAF Base on the outskirts of Cape Town. There was a train service to Cape Town from the naval base at Simonstown. This we boarded at Camp Retreat. The Royal Navy had a mascot on their strength. It was a huge hound called Happy. Now this dog's duty was to patrol the corridor train to make sure that the drunken sailors were woken up and escorted off the train. Good old Happy learned to do the same for the drunken airmen at our stop. I visited the renowned Snake Park and cable car. There was also a roller skating rink at Wynberg.

Meusemburg was a beautiful seaside resort for the white inhabitants. When we embarked aboard the *Stratheden* which had been converted into a troop ship, it was loaded with army personnel returning with their families from a tour of duty in India. We were therefore allocated to decks well below the waterline.

When we put out to sea, the RAF soon learned to pitch our hammocks on the upper deck. The main drawback to this was that early every morning the deck hands sluiced and scrubbed the deck. We became very adept at unslinging our hammocks before we were drowned in seawater from the hosepipes. Anything was better than sleeping down in the 'hold'.

Another dodgy thing on a troop ship was the toilet fa-cilities. A complete deck was converted to accommodate communal toilets. These toilet seats were placed in rows of about ten and boxed in. Underneath the seats was a trough of flushing water. That would have been OK if the ship remained stationery, but in practice as the ship rolled from side to side in heavy seas, the flushing water would tip over at the ends of the trough and soon you would be paddling in it. There was always a wag who would roll up a ball of paper, set it alight and send it sailing along the gulley under our seats. Consequently, there were several singed buttocks among the squatters. The rows of seats were spaced too closely for comfort and it was most embarrassing facing one another with your knees almost touching those in front. It was a job to appear nonchalant. All that was missing to make it a complete misery was the shackles around our ankles, like convicts would have.

Washing and shaving were in a similar vein. There was a very limited space in which to perform one's ablutions, and to get to a mirror for shaving purposes was almost mission impossible. I got quite adept at shaving by touch. When you decided to take a shower, it was in salt water. A special soap was provided for this purpose. This left you all sticky and was hardly worth the effort.

When we arrived at Gibraltar we dropped anchor out in the bay. Only a few of the privileged ones were allowed to go ashore. When they were on the gangplank a disgruntled repatriated soldier emptied his billycan of tea over them from the top deck. What a panic ensued, but by the time it took to reach the top deck the culprit had vanished and the pursuers had to return empty handed. I presume these favoured few went ashore like tourists to see the sights and to view the renowned 'Barbary apes'. There was no black-out on Gibraltar, it being pointless as their near neighbours, Spain, were so-called neutral. That was a bit of a laugh, because they harboured Italian one- and two-men submarines. Whilst we were anchored in the bay a Royal Navy destroyer had to circle our ship occasionally dropping a depth charge to deter the aforesaid submarines.

Below deck, my hammock was slung adjacent to the riveted steel plates of the ship's hull. Our deck was below the waterline, subsequently, every time a depth charge exploded within close proximity of our ship, the pressure forced the rivets to leak. What with the noise and all, I did not get much sleep. We had to endure this for a week while waiting to join a convoy of ships coming through the Suez Canal. I think a few of us, given the opportunity, would have jumped ship and to hell with the consequences. I was very relieved to get under way again. We had the captured

Italian battleship – *Garibaldi* – in our convoy. After six weeks at sea with one or two scary moments when we were spotted by an enemy Fokka Wolf airplane, we eventually sailed up the River Clyde to Greenock in Scotland.

After throwing our sun helmets into the Clyde, we were expecting a welcome home. Not a bit of it. When we finally disembarked into the gloom of a typical Scottish winter's day, we had to unload our own kit bags because the dockers were on strike. There were red flags flying everywhere. You could imagine them doing that in Russia.

At least now we were on terra firma; at last we could sleep on a proper bed, not a hammock. On the ship, a whole deck had been taken over to sling these hammocks – there were about a hundred of these – row after row, with barely a foot between each. Some of us would go to the galley to cadge a piece of boxwood to use as a spreader to open up the top end of the hammock. At night time, when we tried to get some sleep, there was always someone who needed to go to the toilet. This meant that he had to try and squeeze by in the gap between the hammocks. Seeing as how the only illumination was from a low powered blue bulb, this had often set the hammocks swinging, which had a knock on effect. During the evening we had been allowed to go up on the upper deck. We would use this occasion to go up and get a drag on a fag. We had to be very careful to shield the glowing cigarette because an unshielded one could be seen for a long distance, and would put the convoy in danger from the enemy.

After disembarking at Greenock, we entrained to Morecambe, a seaside town in Lancashire. Upon arrival we were allocated to be billeted with several landladies. We were starving by now and what a pleasant surprise awaited us. Yes, you've guessed it, a plateful of the renowned fish and chips. These we hadn't tasted for four years. I think the landladies were delighted to cater for us, it being off-season in December. We had not much to do except attend roll call in the morning to make sure nobody absconded. After a few exercises down on the front the rest of the day was ours to make the most of. After about a week of this heaven, we were posted to our various squadrons.

I was posted to a Lancaster Bomber Base in Lincolnshire, not all that far from the City of Lincoln. The only snag was that we were so busy that we only had one day off in ten days. One day I was told to make my way to Cosford near Wolverhampton. This was a technical training camp. During my four years absence from England there were many modifications to aero engines, both inline and radial. I needed to catch up with the latest developments. At the end of this course was an examination paper to be completed.

I was enjoying myself here and was not keen to return to the one day in ten leisure time. Being friendly with my instructor, he told me that one way of avoiding this was to ask for another week's revision, and from there I would be put into the 'the pool' and take my chances as to where I would be posted. This I did. Not a bad decision. I was posted to No. 3. OADU (Overseas Aircraft Dispersal Unit) Station at Hurn Aerodrome near Christchurch, Hampshire. There was a lot of activity going on leading up to the invasion of France. Bournemouth was teeming with American troops awaiting embarkation. They were very generous to us 'Limey airmen' throwing cartons of fifty cigarettes from the upstairs windows of their civilian billets to us. These were very welcome because our 'fag ration' was small.

Everyone was confined to camp for the twenty-four hour period prior to D-Day – invasion of Europe. Our aerodrome was directly opposite the invasion zone. Our particular unit was put on permanent duty crew. Part of our duty was to refuel and rearm the planes as required by the invading Forces. The planes were as varied as the situation demanded. On the day of the invasion, I attended to a small private plane, either a Proctor or an Auster. The pilot was a general who had been over the other side of the Channel to see how the battle was progressing. He, not knowing the correct RAF procedure after refuelling, asked for me to hand swing the propeller, but had the throttle wide open, whereupon the plane moved forward. I noticed this out of the corner of my eye and instinctively dived forward under the main plane, thus avoiding being minced up by the propeller. When the pilot realised what he had done, thinking he had killed me, he was as white as a sheet and full of apologies. Now this must be the first time an airman had got away with calling a general a 'stupid bastard'. He should have had his brakes on and he was too impatient for me to use 'chocks' under the wheels.

Another dodgy day was when my rigger and I had to re-fuel a Mosquito Fighter Bomber. We had the fuel bowser pulled up to the nose of the aircraft and proceeded to refuel. I sent my rigger to climb up into the cockpit to watch the fuel gauge and let me know when to cease the flow of juice. Unbeknown to us was the fact that covering the control column firing button was the pilot's helmet gear. Yes, the button had been left in the firing position and my mate had barely touched it, a sharp 'zipp' of cannon fire sent shells whizzing on either side of me. I was placed nicely on top of the bowser by the nose. One yard either side and I would have been cut in half. Another lucky factor was the angle at which the aircraft rested. A lesser angle and the shells would have smashed into the fuel tanker and the whole bloody lot would have gone up. After the inquiry it was revealed that the aircraft shells had landed on a distant farm, destroying a couple of farm buildings.

As the war progressed, so our casualties increased. The American Air Force had a squadron of Dakota transport planes operating out of RAF Lynham in Wiltshire. Now these sixty planes were on a shuttle service to France bringing back casualties and returning with ammo and jerry cans of fuel. They were getting snowed under with work. Volunteers were needed to give them some respite. After arriving we soon got stuck in. We just grabbed some sleep and grub where and when we could. We were no strangers to these conditions; they were part of our duty crew mode of living. Directly a Dakota landed, the Yanks piled out and were soon immersed in a game of crap – some dice game. The piles of dollars soon mounted. One day they threw away a large York ham just because there were a few maggots wriggling about on it. We RAF boys soon devoured it.

At a later date, our complete unit was to be transferred from RAF Hurn to RAF Talbeny, Carmarthenshire in West Wales. Volunteers were needed to rough ride it in a convoy of lorries with all our gear in the two-day journey to Wales, the rest to go by train. I was always game for a laugh. We stayed overnight at some RAF camp, and during the early morning resumption of the journey, we went through some sleepy Welsh mining villages. The inhabitants thought they were being invaded, until they realised it was only English invaders, nothing to worry about.

Upon arrival, we had a meal and soon settled into our allotted Nissen huts. It did not take us long to find out where the NAAFI was and to sample Welsh beer. Neither did it take me long to select a nice little NAAFI girl. With all my charm, how could she resist? She did up to a point, until we eventually got married.

As the war progressed, the bombing of Germany intensified. Our American allies used mainly Flying Fortress and Super Forts. The RAF used mainly Lancasters, Stirlings and Halifaxes. The USAF was taking a huge amount of casualties. One contributory factor was that their planes were powered by engines with exhaust superchargers. On night raids, these glowed brightly giving the Germans an easy target to shoot at. It was decided to use them for daylight bombing raids, leaving the RAF to do the night shift because we did not have that problem. A corporal and I were sent to the American airbase at Burtonwood to attend a course and gather the data on these exhaust superchargers. One evening on our free time we palled up with an American airman and went into town. We bumped into a group of nurses and got invited to their quarters. A good time was had by all. So good, in fact, that the three of us failed to return to camp at 23.59 hours as required. Consequently we were charged and sentenced, in my case seven days confined to camp, the Yank got fourteen days, and my corporal friend received a severe reprimand. Same crime; different punishments. At the end of the course came the usual examination. My corporal and I received the highest marks of the entry. It was gratifying to beat our American allies.

Most RAF stations are well dispersed and it is an advantage to obtain a station bicycle. One of my mates could not ride a bike, so I taught him. I got him nicely balanced and held him upright by holding his saddle. Next thing I told him, never look down, just aim the bike at a distant tree and off we go. Unbeknown to him I let go of the saddle and he was away. Unfortunately, I never gave him braking instructions. The tree he was aiming for took care of that.

Whilst at this camp, another incident comes to mind. It was a severe winter and most of the airfields were snowbound. Some of our aircraft returning from a mission were desperate to find a landing strip. Ours was the only field available. So all the airmen were formed up in squads and were sent doubling up and down to compact the snow into a landing strip. Nice little warming up exercise. Good effort though.

There was cause for celebration at the news of VE (Victory in Europe). There was also apprehension as to my future when I was posted overseas again. There would be increased activity against Japan. The fanatical suicide kamikazes would not surrender without a fight. Not knowing when and if I would return from this posting, I applied for a special licence to get married. My little NAAFI girl agreed to my proposal. My two best friends accompanied us up to Llanelli, her home town, to meet her parents, get a ring and tie the knot. The ever-gallant Ernie was making provision for her should anything happen to him.

Our honeymoon was one night's stay at a friend's holiday shack on the cliffs of Broadhaven. Then back to duty the next day.

In the darkest days of the war, Britain stood alone against the Axis Powers, before America was forced to join us because of the Japanese attack on Pearl Harbour. We were suffering a great loss of shipping from U-boat attacks. Britain came to an agreement with the USA to lease to them several British bases for ninety-nine years in exchange for sixty 3-funnelled old destroyers that had been mothballed. One of the main bases was Bermuda. The Yanks very shrewdly joined the biggest islands together by dredging the coral sands, compacting them and thus making Kindley Field Air Base.

Our group were sent to operate a string of staging posts heading towards the Far East. First of all we embarked on a troop ship from Liverpool to Canada. As we sailed up the St Laurence River to Quebec we were given a Twenty Gun Salute, mainly because the ship carried Canadian Servicemen returning home for repatriation. Upon disembarkation the RAF personnel entrained for RCAF Lachine. Once there we were split up into units, my unit consisting of one officer, one sergeant, two corporals and half a dozen fitters and riggers. We were flown to Bermuda to operate a staging post at Kindley Field. We were billeted with the Yanks who treated us very well. We had only to ring up the Watch Tower and request the gasoline tanker for us to refuel our aircraft and it was sent straight away.

On the Base was the PX American for Post Exchange. This was the equivalent to our NAAFI except that whereas the NAAFI were very limited for supplies, you could purchase almost anything very cheaply. No rationing of beer or fags or grub, etc.

We rang up the Watch Tower daily to find out if any RAF planes were expected. Sometimes the answer was negative; this meant we had free time. We would go in our Jeep over to the other side of the island where we had a RAF Rescue Launch manned by a native Bermudian. He very obligingly took us out shark fishing. Other times we could go swimming within an area protected with shark repellent nets. We had a raft anchored within this area which we could swim to. One day when I was leisurely swimming, something grabbed my side, which I struck off by my side-stroke action. I must have broken all records to reach dry land. Upon inspection, my side was a mass of red sucker marks, probably caused by an octopus. Sometimes we went beach combing for seashells, etc. One day we visited a tourist attraction of underground caves. We were asked to sign the visitors' book. On the previous page was the signature of His Royal Highness the Duke of Windsor, Governor of the Bahamas, previously named King Edward VIII. He was uncrowned because of his abdication in favour of his brother George.

We were prepared for a long war against the Japanese, when out of the blue the Yanks dropped two atomic bombs, thus bringing the war to an abrupt end. This saved countless lives, including those of the Japs.

In December that year, our little unit was flown in a Liberator Bomber back to our base in Montreal. On Christmas Day the same plane was assigned to take us back to the UK. After a couple of hours into the flight we, very conveniently, had engine trouble. This necessitated us having to return to Canada and spend Christmas Day enjoying all the goodies instead of ingesting the meagre rations in poor old Blighty. Next day we managed to get to Ayr in Scotland. From there it was a short trip in a Dakota to Blackbush in southern England. At this station we were given a meal of sorts and sleeping accommodation in a Nissen hut. Unfortunately this had been empty for a long time without heat from the usual pot-bellied stove. All the blankets were damp and we were unable to scrounge any firewood or coal. The next day, we were given a forty-eight hour pass and told to report for duty at RAF Henlow. I paid my mother a visit and several members of my family. I was at a very low ebb and an easy target for the flu bug, what with me coming from the warmth of Bermuda to the sub-zero temperatures of Canada and the cold and damp of British winter. My sister-in-law very kindly bundled my kitbag and the rest of my equipment in a pram and got me to Richmond Railway Station. I can't quite remember getting from there to RAF Henlow. The next day I reported sick and was immediately rushed to hospital with the flu turning to pneumonia and a reoccurrence of malaria. After surviving the rigours of war, it looked like I was to succumb to an ordinary illness. In my hospital bed and in my fever, I was reduced to seven stone in weight. Floating in and out of consciousness and delirium I had a crisis in the middle of the night and the medical officer was called to my bedside. All of a sudden I sat bolt upright and brought up all the offending filth in my chest: crisis over! I was given some sick leave and then told to report to West Kirby for demobilisation. After turning down the offer of re-enlisting, me being a regular airman, I was kitted out with a demob suit, given all the monies owing to me and thought that it was civvy street for me; but not quite. I had to serve a further twenty-one days that I owed them for the twenty-one days AWOL in Rhodesia.

Now for the monotony of civilian life, but not if I have anything to do with it.

After a couple of weeks into my demob leave, I was getting a bit restless in civvy street, with no action. I decided to go to Heathrow Airport and see what was on offer. BOAC (the British Overseas Airways Company) offered me a job servicing their fleet of Lancastrians and Yorks, which were civilian adaptations of Lancaster Bombers. The York was made with a wide fuselage for cargo whilst the Lancastrian was adapted to carry passengers. This job would have suited me down to the ground having worked on 'Lancs' during the war. Unfortunately, the vacancy was not at Heathrow but at Hurn Airport, the one I mentioned before whilst in the RAF. I could not commute daily from Richmond to Bournemouth so reluctantly I turned the job down. Little did I know that BOAC's staff would be transferred from Hurn to Heathrow and be housed in accommodation built for them with the co-operation of the council. That is the way the cookie crumbles, as the Yanks say. No good grumbling, get on with it.

When I was on a bus, I noticed an advert for fitters to work on buses at the Chiswick Bus Depot. There were about fifty applications for six jobs. After an interview, one of the jobs was mine. They thought I would be over the moon at being one of the lucky ones. Not so, when I learned that the wage was to be £5 per week less stoppages. I had to turn it down because a quarter of the £5 was needed to pay for my rent.

Eventually I had to accept a job for the going rate of £5 per week with the North Thames Gas Board repairing their fleet of vehicles at Brentford. I could manage with that plus overtime. My wife, Vera, God bless her was prepared to do a few hours as a charlady, or in today's jargon, 'domestic assistant'. I put my name down on the Council's waiting list for a council house. There was a points system for applicants. I got points for my war service and Vera got points for NAAFI service and should have got points for our living accommodation. Not being worldly wise enough to accentuate the misery of living in our damp semi-basement room by hanging a clothes line above the bed, Vera – being very house proud – kept it neat and tidy. When the Housing Officer came around to view our accommodation and assess points, she remarked that we seemed comfortable. Bang goes our position from the top of the list, never to be considered again as in need. By the way, these semi-basement flats were condemned before the war as being uninhabitable, but were reprieved because of the shortage of housing after the war.

I joined a group of would-be self-help builders. Our group was made up of fifty various tradesmen plus a surveyor and architect. Once a week we met in a pub aptly named the Bricklayers Arms to discuss things, such as how to obtain a progressive mortgage, and the minimum hours to be put in by each of us in the construction of our dream homes. As it turned out, it was only a dream because any available building sites were duly given to a prospective builder who no doubt was a member of the Freemasons. We got no help whatsoever from the Tory Council, unlike all the Labour Councils, who fell over backwards to assist these self-help groups and to make building sites available to them. After a year when we were all getting skilled at bricklaying etc, we had to disband owing to no co-operation from the council.

The next thing I tried was to go squatting in the disused army huts adjacent to Richmond Park. They soon put a stop to that idea by staving in the roofs, making them uninhabitable. How dare we have the audacity to squat in Richmond! We heard through the grapevine that the Yanks were abandoning their wartime base in Bushey Park. When we got there we were just pipped at the post to occupy the last vacant Nissen hut. These squatters were very lucky because the Yanks came back during the Cold War and they were all allocated council houses.

I became very desperate when Vera announced that she was pregnant. There was no such thing as the pill in those days. I think the Lord above took pity on me and led me to find a vacant flat over the shops in York Street, Twickenham, in time to bring my wife and son a home to come to. Although this was not ideal, at least it was three empty rooms and a roof over our heads. I managed to get two rickety second hand chairs to replace the two wooden boxes to sit on, a table of sorts and a put-u-up bed/sofa. A cot for the baby and we were all set. I had it all worked out, but you know about the 'best laid plans of mice and men'?

First of all the baby was due to be born in the middle of March and I would receive about £50 tax rebate. This would enable me to buy a cot, a pram and all the baby requirements. He was three weeks overdue when he was dragged out forcibly with a pair tongs in Kingston Hospital. Poor Vera who had all the pain. Poor Ernie who had lost the £50 rebate by two days. Another big shock I had when I visited my wife in hospital was when I was informed that my son had been born with a split uvula in the roof of his mouth. This meant he was unable to suck a teat. Milk had to be expressed from his mother with a breast pump into a container and from there spoon-fed to the baby every two hours. To make matters worse – if possible – they had forgotten to remove the afterbirth, which meant that poor Vera had to be reopened and restitched. After a few days I was allowed to take my wife and baby home.

Now the real trial began. What with the lack of sleep by this baby's feeding process and having to cycle to work in Brentford I was beginning to feel the strain. After a while, mother's milk ran out, so I bought a baby feeding bottle, a boat shaped bottle with a teat at one end and a valve at the other. Bearing in mind the baby could not suck, I got a red-hot needle and enlarged the teat hole and rigged up a sort of drip feed into his mouth. This innovation worked very well and took a lot of pressure off us both. The milk mixture was the 'National Dried', and baby was thriving well and we soon had a bonny bouncing boy.

In my ignorance I had been feeding him with the full-strength milk powder, instead of the half-strength. Nobody told me there were two kinds. Anyway, with that and wartime orange juice, he survived. When he was one year old, he was given a plastic surgery operation in St Thomas' Hospital, Westminster to repair the uvula. I am delighted to say the operation was a complete success and now he can talk normally. Whereas, but for the operation, he would have had an impediment to his speech.

During the war and for some years afterwards there was not only food rationing, but rationing for anything in short supply. Clothing coupons and dockets were issued for such items as curtains, bed sheets, etc. I was allowed to buy curtains for one room only in my flat. Never mind, I scrounged some old blackout material for the other two rooms I rigged up a pulley system and clothes line out of the rear kitchen window to save Vera having to walk up and down three flights of stairs to the yard below to hang out the washing. My old RAF kitbag came in very handy, I could cycle home with it full of coke, for sixpence, on my crossbar. There would be frequent electrical power cuts and people would have to use oil lamps and candles to illuminate their dwellings. This was not for Ernie & Co; I again scrounged a swan necked gas bracket to fix to the wall near our gas stove. It was a simple job for me to connect a gas supply from the stove to gas lamp. Now all I needed was a gas mantle – and lo and behold, I could dispense with the candles. I quite enjoyed this battle for survival. I could live up to my RAF motto, *Per ardua ad astra²*. I always accepted a challenge to my competence to survive.

Vera wanted to show off our bonny baby to her family in Llanelly, South Wales. It was a hot sunny day when we set out. All that changed when we got over the border into Wales on the train. It was rainy and it rained ever day whilst we were there. We were glad when our two week visit was over. In a café by Llanelly Railway Station, prior to boarding a train to London, I asked the proprietor if I could buy a cup of milk for our thirsty baby. He declined saying he needed the milk for his customers. May he rot in hell.

So much for our visit to 'the land of our fathers'. In the words of Harry Secombe, 'we'll keep a welcome in the hillside' – ha ha. When our train pulled into Cardiff station for a ten minute stop so that people could change trains, I was out like a shot and fought my way to the front of the queue at the Station Buffet and got my mug of milk just in time before the train resumed the journey to Paddington. Upon arrival we managed to get a meal in a café. The best meal we had eaten for two weeks. Needless to say it would be a very long time before we visited Wales again. In the meantime, London had been basking in sunshine. For several years we welcomed the Welsh relatives to our meagre abode in Twickenham.

I worked eight and a half years for the Gas Company and became a co-partner after the first year. This meant two pence an hour increase. During this period I earned a pat on the back and £10 for inventing a tool to speed up the relining of the clutch. Another device was a way to obviate the necessity of removing the cab of a lorry for maintenance work. No remuneration for this although the man-hours saved were considerable. When the fleet of lorries had been

---

² Through struggles to the stars.

renewed, our overtime was stopped. I was reluctant to hand in my notice, but I could not cope with the reduction in my wages. I learned later that my action induced the management to reintroduce overtime to the delight of my former workmates.

Having scrimped and scraped for these years, I managed the down payment on the purchase of a rundown semi. Another thing – after a struggle we managed to get Trade Union recognition. This put into action a fair balance between worker and the Bosses Union CBI.

I modified my bicycle to receive a mini motor over the rear wheel. This 49cc engine took the load off my pedal power. I fitted a back peddling brake, put tandem spokes and a heavy duty tyre to the rear wheel and I was mechanised. I failed my first driving test on it because the MOT tester was inebriated, endeavouring to keep warm on this December day with the intake of whiskey. He failed everyone on this day. He got the sack. I passed at the next attempt. This licence enabled me to drive my three-wheeled Reliant Robin providing that I had to 'blank off' the reverse gear. Vera and I had some of the best years of our lives driving around Britain in it. I never did blank off the reverse gear. Another economy measure I took when our baby was born, I purchased a nine-inch television set. I got it for £40 cheaply, because it was a demonstration model, relieved of purchase tax. There were not many people around in those early days who had a set to receive such broadcasts as the Queen's coronation and Churchill's funeral.

I needed more money so I got myself a job with BOAC at Heathrow. This suited me fine, being shift work, allowing me to spend a lot of time knocking my old semi into shape. Again my old kitbag came in useful. There was a severe shortage of fuel one winter. There was a mountain in reserve of coke at Heathrow, some of which found its way mysteriously into my kitbag and from there on to my crossbar to be transported to my dwelling place, thereby enabling me to keep wife and child warm enough to survive.

I enjoyed working twenty-five years for BOAC. This semi-detached house I was trying to purchase was in such a bad state of repair that neither the council nor Building Society would give me a mortgage. I suggested to the owner that he could advance me the money for a two year period at 5 per cent interest to enable me to get the place up to a standard acceptable to a Building Society for a mortgage. He agreed because he was only holding the property in trust. Now it was up to me to get on with the work. First of all I had to tackle the problem of dry rot and woodworm. A bit awkward because timber was still in short supply. I overcame this by ripping the diseased wood out and replaced it with concrete on top of a membrane for a damp course. So far, so good.

These old houses had outdoor lavatories, but who wanted to venture out on cold days to sit on the throne? Right, the answer to this was to bash out the brickwork adjacent to the toilet and build a lean-to extension encompassing said toilet. Next job was to replace all the old type sash windows with plate glass louvered ones and new sills. A bit of painting and wallpapering, then a Building Society was happy to grant me a mortgage. This was well in time for me to beat the two year deadline imposed upon me by the former owner. Now at last after ten years waiting for a council house I was able to tell them in no uncertain terms what to do with their Points Scheme. In this day and age an immigrant can be given housing accommodation within ten weeks.

One of the rooms to my old house had a flat roof which frequently leaked. I ripped off the offending perforated zinc and replaced it with heavy duty hard board and roofing felt.

It defied the elements for over twenty years. Not bad for an amateur.

Another venture was to design and lay a crazy paved flower garden to the front of the house. The council delivered a ton of broken paving stones for this purpose.

Near to where I lived was a retirement home for elderly entertainments people called Brinsworth House. When they sold off part of their substantial grounds for house building, the ganger in charge of demolishing unwanted outbuildings sold me the old Cucumber House. I very carefully removed all the fourteen-inch by forty-inch panes of glass from the glazing bars and transported them to my abode. I used a one-wheeled barrow for this purpose. At the end of my street was a small garage, and I stopped there to borrow an oilcan to lubricate my wheel which had developed a squeak. To my horror when I took my hands off the barrow the bloody lot capsized and bang went a load of my carefully retrieved glass. Fortunately, there was still sufficient glass for me to build a fourteen foot greenhouse in the rear garden.

I am not all that clever because when Vera had to go into hospital I decided to do the weekly washing. I bunged the lot, underwear, towels etc into the washing machine. Unfortunately, the whole lot was dyed blue. Good job the shirt was blue and not one of my red ones. Conclusion? I am not such a clever lad after all!

Part Three
Ernie's Dad

THIS NARRATIVE IS a sequel to own story, since Ernie's dad was only briefly mentioned. This was mainly due to the fact that a man takes second place to the matriarch in a family home: she was the hub around which the whole family orbited. In my youth, she was often referred to as 'Her Indoors,' which described her role in life. In order to be fair, the father should have been dubbed 'Him Outdoors' as he was mainly outdoors earning money to keep the family from starving. We only saw Dad for comparatively short periods whilst Mum was always at home for us all. Dad's main pleasure in life, when he wasn't working, was to down a few pints of beer with his pals in the local pub. They would play games of drafts, dominoes, skittles or bar billiards – or play a game of cards for a small stake. Their other main pastime was to select a horse to win a race at favourable odds, or if the price was right, speculate a 'tenner each way' for a place bet. These bets were written down on a slip of paper and signed with a nom de plume such as 'Mickey Mouse' or 'Donald Duck', in fact anything that you fancied. Together with the money, the slips would be passed to a bookie's runner. This was all underhand, as gambling was illegal except on the racecourse itself. Nowadays, there are legalised betting shops.

Another way to get around the gambling laws was to bet on a selection of football game results. This scheme was called 'football fools', invented by Moores Brothers. Originally, they were printed in newspapers, in which you filled in your selections, cut out the section and sent it with your remuneration to the promoters. To get around the gambling laws, you sent your money a week in arrears. If you failed to honour your bet you were blacklisted. You had to be very careful filling in these newspaper football coupons, because the ink of your pen would run on this absorbent material. Ballpoint pens had not yet been invented. Necessity being the mother of invention, the quill pen progressed to the metal pen nib, and from then to the invention of the fountain pen. When a pilot of an aeroplane flying at a high altitude was making an entry on his kneepad paper, his fountain pen would burst due to atmospheric pressures. Thus the Biro and the Schaeffer ballpoint pens were invented. But I digress.

Dad showed me three of the old fivers that he had won gambling on the aforementioned football pools. Provided he could earn enough money to pay for his gambling, beer and 'baccy' he was a contented man, bless him. He was a tough man. He needed to be, during those years of the slump after the First World War. I suspect that during his early childhood he may have been tormented over his speech impediment – a hereditary defect. Perhaps he resorted to fisticuffs, which hardened him up. In later years, persons afflicted with this ailment were successfully given plastic surgery to alleviate the problem.

When Dad was demobbed at the end of the First World War (in which he served as a soldier taking care of horses and mules in the East Surrey Regiment), he came home to the so-called 'country for heroes'. That was a joke – he came home to unemployment and very near starvation. After a while a liberal, named Beverage, came up with an idea called 'the dole', but as far as I know he could not wait for that. He rolled up his sleeves, bought a ladder, bucket, chamois leather and scrim cloth to start a window cleaning round. This ladder was a very heavy one, made of wood – aluminium ladders had not yet been invented. To supplement his income from window cleaning, he got himself a job at his local newsagent's delivering a heavy barrow load of newspapers and magazines on a large paper round. Previous to me getting my own paper round at the age of eleven, I used to assist him on Sundays, as, on that day, the load was the greatest of the week. This was good training for me. Anyway, we were both grateful to have a job at all.

Dad lived in an era when men took pride in their appearance. Their spouses made sure their man was turned out 'spick and span' from head to toe. Hair was meticulously combed and plastered down with hair cream, side burns and moustaches neatly trimmed. Men always had a clean shirt collar, cufflinks etc, a handkerchief showing out of the jacket top pocket, maybe a flower in the top button hole, a pocket watch and chain and fob in their waistcoat pockets; a sharp crease in the trousers and highly polished shoes. This turnout was their Sunday best suit, reserved for weekends, weddings, funerals, christenings, etc. Most of this gear was often taken on a Monday morning to Uncles', the local pawnbroker, to get a cash loan on a pledge to be redeemed on Friday's payday. Every town had its pawnshop, easily recognised by the three brass balls hanging over the shop door. Likewise, a red and white-bandaged pole represented a barber's shop. The reason for this being that barbers often had to do minor surgery, such as cutting off a badly damaged finger etc. Maybe they were places that did not have a resident doctor to attend. Most of the old shop signs are now a thing of the past.

Dad had a younger brother who thought it was his patriotic duty to enlist in the army to fight for 'King and Country'. Being under-aged (the minimum age limit to join up was eighteen years), he falsified his age and was allowed to enlist in the East Surrey Regiment. He was one of the cannon fodder, mown down in France shortly after his enlistment. He won a medal, awarded posthumously.

Let's get back to a lighter theme: on Saturdays, we had a market in Church Street, which was quite a lively place. All the market stalls were illuminated with lamps; some were oil lamps, others were naphtha flares. There was plenty of chatter and good humour from the stallholders, and at around about 11 p.m. they practically threw all their perishable items at you. Don't forget that we had no fridges so the stuff would soon go rotten if not quickly consumed.

Most pubs at chuck-out time invariably had a punch-up outside to the enjoyment of the spectators. To add to this merry scene, the 'Sally Army' would be banging away on their tambourines and singing, 'Come and Join Us'. They had done alright selling their 'Young Soldier' pamphlets to the generous, half-cut drinkers. Perhaps they would save our souls on Sunday?

Regatta time in the summer outside of the Barmy Arms pub by the embankment of the River Thames was quite pleasant. Apart from the pub we had a small fair and fireworks display. You could try your luck to reach the leg of lamb at the end of a greasy pole, or maybe fall off into the river – good fun! A man named Cockles would go down some steps into the Thames with a handmade diver's helmet on. He relied on us lads to pump air to him with a foot pump, then he would light fireworks to give us a display. He was a bit of an oddball, but what the heck? All part of life's tapestry.

In a pub or hotel there were several rooms all of which

had their own peculiar atmosphere. There would be the public bar nicknamed 'the Spit and Sawdust'; the reason for this was the fact that the floor was strewn with sawdust to soak up the spilt beer. The 'spit' was derived from the provision of a brass spittoon for the benefit of tobacco chewers whose saliva had to be released. The chewers became quite adept at spitting into a spittoon from a distance. A man would have a block of rum-soaked, compressed tobacco from which a sliver would be shaved off using his penknife. The waistcoat pockets were very handy for carrying such items as snuffboxes, watches, cigarette papers, matches, etc. Snuff was a very fine powder similar to ground pepper which was ground up from tobacco stalks and had the same property of making one sneeze. Once a man had opened his snuffbox, it was proffered to his surrounding company, as were cigarettes. You would take a small pinch, place it on the back of your hand and sniff it up and this would inevitably make you sneeze and your eyes water. You might ask, Why should anybody want to sneeze? Good question – the act of sneezing was to clear your head and chest of all the foul air you had breathed. There was plenty of foul air in those days, what with all the fires and train engines belching out smoke. In recent times, smokeless zones were introduced: there were saloon bars, lounge rooms, private rooms, 'snugs' for the ladies to meet, chat and scandalise in general. Even in larger establishments there were reading rooms in which one could obtain a book or newspaper to read. There was also the Bottle and Jug, an off-license bar where people could get a jug filled up with beer for home use. From factories, a lad would be sent out to fetch beer. He would carry a wooden rod along which were suspended covered mugs, ideal for this purpose.

By law, a price list had to be displayed in a prominent position in the public bar – supplied by the brewery – so that whatever pub you used the price was standard. This did not apply to other bars, the reason being that the landlord could be recompensed for the expenditure of providing amenities such as carpets, ashtrays and an indoor toilet as opposed to an outside one.

Pubs in more recent times did away with public bars so that they could charge the customers any price that they could get away with. Women were not encouraged to frequent public bars because when one appeared on the scene the men, being gentlemen, had to curb their tongues from uttering foul language. The few ladies that smoked in those days mainly puffed away at the end of a long cigarette holder. Most men in the public bar rolled their own fags whilst 'gentlemen' bought 'tailor mades' packaged in fives, tens or twenties. Most cigarette manufacturers encouraged you to smoke more then was good for your health by putting coupons into those packs, which you could trade for articles such as a watch or even a gramophone. Mind you, to get such items you had to smoke like a chimney. Other manufacturers gave cigarette cards which were very popular among young lads who saved up sets of fifty. There were sets of such things as football teams, soldiers, trains, butterflies, animals, etc. There was a lot of swapping going on and card games in school playing yards to add enjoyment to their young lives.

These catchpenny schemes were designed to induce folk to part with their money instead of putting it away for a rainy day – these savings were called 'mouldy money'.

Coffee houses were another meeting place popular with those who did not wish to drink alcoholic beverages. Many a business deal was transacted in such establishments.

I must pause for a while with this narrative – it being the sixtieth anniversary of VE Day against Germany – to reflect upon and to raise a glass to my fellow men at arms, whether they be dead or still living. Sixty years ago, I remember that although the war in Europe was at an end, there was still the battle to be won against the Japanese. But for the timely intervention of the American atomic bombs, the war would undoubtedly have dragged on for a long time and many more lives would have been lost, both Allied and, paradoxically, Japanese as well.

As I have mentioned, at that VE time I was to marry my little Welsh NAAFI girl by special license, prior to being posted overseas again.

Anyway, where was I? Oh, now I remember, about Dad. Apart from being a tough man he was also good looking. No wonder Mum could not resist his advances – hence the production of our large family.

Dad would take his ladder and stride along the riverside Ducks Walk into Richmond to clean the windows of a pub for a few bob. One hot day in the summertime he had a well-earned glass of cider for refreshment. Unfortunately, the heat got to him and he collapsed. When the police arrived, they assumed, wrongly, that he was drunk. He was carried away to spend the night in the police cells. They did not have the decency to inform Mum who was sick with worry at his absence. In the morning, the police surgeon immediately recognised the symptoms of a stroke and rushed him off to hospital. At this time, I was serving in Africa. Mum kept this to herself in order not to worry me. It was not until I returned to England that I was informed. Dad's stroke had left him paralysed all down one side.

No doubt, had I been informed, I would have called someone to account for this diabolical action. It was far too late now to seek redress. In these days, Mum would have received compensation for the loss of Dad's earnings. On another occasion the police 'pinched' Dad for being a bookies' runner. That's a misnomer, as Dad could hardly walk as a result of his stroke. Dad was only trying to earn a bob or two so that he could buy some tobacco for his only pleasure. You could say that I was not particularly enamoured with the police. Another thing that got my back up was when the police pinched me for parking my three wheeled reliant in the approach to a pedestrian crossing, despite the fact that this crossing was at the widest part of the road at Twickenham junction. I was an easy target for Plod the policeman, who was eager to get promotion for his zealous actions.

After I had pleaded guilty – as I undoubtedly was – the friendly woman Magistrate fined me £3 and endorsed my license for three years.

In the bad old days of the depression, the main topic of conversation was work, or rather the lack of such. When men met their friends the main greeting was, 'Hi Bill,' or whatever name it was, 'are you working?' There was an influx of Irish workmen, it being pretty bleak back in Ireland. There was friction between them and our own men in England because they were willing to work for ten pence an hour, whereas the going rate for a labourer in England was one shilling per hour. One could not blame the Irishmen, because their motto was, 'Better half a loaf then none.' At this time there was a project to do away with the unsanitary open-sewage system and replace it with a more up-to-date system. To add fuel to the flames of discontent, at the gates of the contractor's establishment was a notice: 'ONLY IRISHMEN NEED APPLY'.

Naturally there was more profit when using cheap labour.

Another bone of contention was that when England declared war on the Germans, Ireland, being a neutral country, did not have conscription into the armed forces which protected their civilians from enrolment. It's no wonder there were punch-ups on the weekend after the men had a skinful of beer to relieve the tension. No doubt,

Dad was not excluded from this practice – the ancient art of fisticuffs. I'm confident that he could hold his own against an opponent. Dad was very proud to show me off to his friends in the pub when I came home in RAF uniform on my first leave. After all, it was his signature on the enlistment form, which had allowed me to enlist in 1938, the year before the Second World War broke out.

Dad was a shrewd man. Every time his local pub had a darts match to be played, he would volunteer his services as the 'chalk man', and he, being very adept at chalking up the scores very swiftly, invariably got the job. He knew very well that his mug of beer was always topped up. At the finish of a match, the captain of the away team always bought the home team captain a gallon of beer to be doled out to his team, which included the 'chalker'.

Once a year, in summertime, there was always the annual pub outing to look forward to. The men would assemble outside the pub all togged up in their Sunday best outfits, their pockets bulging with their mouldy money saved up all year long to be spent on beer, trinkets and sweet rocks from Southend-on-Sea. When the open-topped charabanc arrived, they would all pile aboard and before very long they would be on their way. Provided they did not have a motor breakdown they would arrive at the halfway house. This is when they would start drinking beer in earnest. By the time they reached Southend, many of them never saw the sea, having to sleep off the effects of alcohol on the nearest park bench. When, at times, they were sober enough to walk along the promenade they would enjoy a plate of cockles, whelks, shrimps or winkles, buy trinkets and sticks of rock and have a good old sing-song in one of the pubs, accompanied on the 'old Joanna' by someone who could tickle the ivories. Then they would get some fish and chips and it was 'all-aboard' to head for home. All of them would be half-cut, singing along the way, and a good time was had by all. There was many a hangover the next morning. Never mind!

Enough for now about Ernie's Dad. It is a pity that I have still been unable to locate a photograph of him. But I have an image of him in my mind. God bless him, may he rest in peace.

Now let's talk about the living…

Part Four
Afterword

FORGIVE ME FOR sounding like a preacher, but let us pause for a moment or two to view the beauties of Mother Nature and to thank her for her gifts of water and the sustenance of life. We are surrounded by her flora and fauna. ('Here endeth the first lesson' – ha, ha.)

You have only to look around everywhere to appreciate what life has to offer, and there is an ever-changing menu to choose from. Every season, she has a surprise packet for our delight. The trouble is that most of us have more things to occupy ourselves with. What with the pleasures of the material world in which we seem to have to keep up with the Joneses in the rat race, we have things that are for the taking.

Right now, I have been listening to the blackbird singing his heart out to attract a female. He has a different song according to the seasons (I am trying to condense in as few words as possible, time being short). Look at the robin redbreast. He is adorned to attract a female to continue the species. Let us not forget man's contribution to the overall picture: man has built bridges, cathedrals, castles, stately homes; created works of art, innumerable items such as the Eiffel Tower in France, The Hanging Gardens of Babylon, pyramids, the Sphinx and many other wonders of the world. How about Sydney Harbour Bridge, the leaning tower of Pisa, the Great Wall of China, or the Statue of Liberty in America? There are so many that the reader will have to research. Forget about all the crap that you view on TV. Be selective; look for programmes that are interesting and more educational. Read more, especially my efforts at expressing myself!

There are such beautiful and interesting places in the UK, that you do not have to go abroad. Keep your money in circulation here at home. Get your priorities right. Literally on your own doorstep are places of interest, such as Kew Gardens, Hampton Court, Windsor Castle... and so on. Further afield are places of note such as Wells Cathedral, Salisbury Cathedral with its leaning spire, York Minster in the centre of York City, entered into through one of its several gates. Visit Cheddar Gorge and Wooky Hole... all the places I have visited. Go now, get your priorities right. Forget about burning your body on beaches contracting skin cancer. Seek out all these interesting places; I am sure you will thoroughly enjoy the experience.

Glossary

All-in wrestling   British wrestling which has very few rules to be observed

Charabanc   early form of tour bus

Chocks   wedge-shaped blocks of wood placed in front of an aeroplane's wheels to prevent it moving

Erk   air force term for the lower ranks

Fuel bowser   a petrol tanker of small size. When working with the Americans second line in Bermuda, we had to use the American terminology 'gasoline wagon'.

Jankers   punishment for serviceman/woman

Old Joanna   piano (*slang*)

Spanish Galleon: a sea creature so named because they are propelled across the surface of the water by the breeze using sail-like fins, thus resembling the Spanish ships.

Sprog   man aspiring to be a pilot

Printed in the United Kingdom
by Lightning Source UK Ltd.
132400UK00001B/20/A